2-24-60

PAPAL PRONOUNCEMENTS ON MARRIAGE AND THE FAMILY

PAPAL PRONOUNCEMENTS ON MARRIAGE AND THE FAMILY

From Leo XIII to Pius XII

(1878-1954)

By

Alvin Werth, O.F.M.Cap., A.M.
Clement S. Mihanovich, Ph.D.

THE BRUCE PUBLISHING COMPANY
MILWAUKEE

IMPRIMI POTEST:

VERY REV. VICTOR GREEN, O.F.M.CAP.
Minister Provincial

NIHIL OBSTAT:

JOHN A. SCHULIEN, S.T.D.
Censor librorum

IMPRIMATUR:

✠ ALBERTUS G. MEYER
Archiepiscopus Milwauchiensis

Die 11a Junii, 1955

Rosary College Dewey Classification Number: 392.5

Library of Congress Catalog Card Number: 55–12375

Introduction

PURPOSE OF THE BOOK

The purpose of this book is to provide a handy means of reference for the pronouncements on marriage and the family made by the popes within the past seventy-five years. Our aim was to locate, analyze, and then group under appropriate headings the pronouncements made from the beginning of the pontificate of Leo XIII (1878) to the year 1954 in the reign of Pius XII.

1104148

DEFINITIONS OF DOCUMENTS QUOTED

The papal pronouncements in this compilation are taken from the encyclicals, allocutions, and addresses of the popes. Of these, encyclical letters

. . . are by far the most familiar to the laity and the ones most widely published and translated. As the term signifies, encyclicals are in form circular letters intended to be passed on from one to another of the group addressed. In actual practice, however, they are addressed to all the bishops of the world, bearing the superscription "to our Venerable Brethren, Patriarchs, Primates, Archbishops, Bishops and other local Ordinaries in peace and communion with the Holy See." The subscription contains the apostolic benediction and a simple date of signature including the year of the pontificate. The pope's name, followed by the contracted form PP. for *Papa*, appears at the foot. When the letters are addressed primarily or entirely not to all the bishops but only to a notable part of the hierarchy they are called *Epistolae Encyclicae* (Encyclical Epistles).

The term "encyclical" has been used by the popes from an early date but it was not commonly adopted before the eighteenth century. Since then it has steadily increased in favor.[1]

---

[1] Sister M. Claudia Carlen, I.H.M., *A Guide to the Encyclicals of the Roman Pontiffs from Leo XIII to the Present Day* (1878–1937) (New York: The H. W. Wilson Company, 1939), pp. 7–8.

INTRODUCTION

A papal allocution is "a solemn form of address, delivered from the throne by the pope to cardinals in a secret consistory."[2] In a less formal sense, a papal allocution includes addresses given to other groups of people. A papal address is a pronouncement of a pope made under various circumstances, including radio broadcasts.[3]

BINDING FORCE OF PAPAL DOCUMENTS

The popes do not normally exercise their infallible teaching office in encyclicals, allocutions, or in addresses; nevertheless, Catholics are not free to ignore their contents. Pope Pius XII, after registering his official disapproval of those who do not take the proper notice of encyclical letters, states:

Nor must it be thought that what is expounded in Encyclical Letters does not of itself demand consent, since in writing such Letters the Popes do not exercise the supreme power of their Teaching Authority. For these matters are taught with the ordinary teaching authority, of which it is true to say: "He who heareth you, heareth me"; and generally what is expounded and inculcated in Encyclical Letters already for other reasons appertains to Catholic doctrine. But if the Supreme Pontiffs in their official documents purposely pass judgment on a matter up to that time under dispute, it is obvious that the matter, according to the mind and will of the same Pontiffs, cannot be any longer considered a question open to discussion among theologians.[4]

In *Catholic Social Principles* by John F. Cronin, S.S., we read:

A careful perusal of the papal writings themselves will show the great authority attached by the popes to encyclicals and other documents. It is common practice for one pope to quote from the writings of another pontiff, and this in such a way as to indicate that these writings are considered binding upon the faithful.

*   *   *

---

[2] *Catholic Dictionary* (published by the Catholic Encyclopedia, 1929), p. 29.

[3] For an illustration of the variety of circumstances under which papal addresses are given, cf. *The National Catholic Almanac for 1953* (Paterson, N. J.: St. Anthony's Guild, 1953), p. 46.

[4] Pope Pius XII, *Humani Generis* (Washington, D. C.: National Catholic Welfare Conference, 1950), p. 10.

Theologians all agree on the broad teaching authority of the pope. This point is well summarized by a French author: "In regard to directives given in an encyclical, while they are not infallible, they nevertheless oblige in conscience, because every Catholic owes an unrestricted and unreserved submission to the exercise of supreme jurisdiction over the universal Church. The Supreme Pontiffs, as is their right, have never used an ordinary encyclical to promulgate an absolute and definitive doctrinal decision. But it does not follow, may we repeat, that the encyclicals do not give directives binding in conscience."

*   *   *

. . . Where the pope is clearly teaching on a matter of divine revelation or natural law, he is acting under the general guidance of the Holy Spirit. His pronouncements may not be solemn definitions, yet it is the part of prudence to assume that this guidance has protected him from error. If a particular teaching appears difficult to accept, there is always the possibility that the reader may have misunderstood the pope. . . . The average Catholic priest or layman should accept doctrinal and moral teachings of the popes.[5]

SOURCES OF INFORMATION

Publications used by the author to locate papal documents are: *Guide to Reference Books;*[6] *An Index to Indexes;*[7] *Acta Apostolicae Sedis* (1909–1953), Volumes I–XLV; *The Guide to Catholic Literature* (1888–1940);[8] *Index to American Catholic Pamphlets;*[9] *A Guide to the Encyclicals of the Roman Pontiffs from Leo XIII to the Present Day* (1878–1937);[10] *Guide to the*

---

[5] John F. Cronin, S.S., *Catholic Social Principles* (Milwaukee: The Bruce Publishing Co., 1950), pp. 56, 58, 59.

[6] Constance M. Winshell, *Guide to Reference Books* (Chicago: American Library Association, 1951), p. 169.

[7] Norma Olin Ireland, *An Index to Indexes* (Boston: The F. W. Faxon Co., 1942), p. 13.

[8] *The Guide to Catholic Literature* (1888–1940) (Detroit, Mich.: Walter Romig and Co.), pp. 664–665.

[9] E. P. Willging, *Index to American Catholic Pamphlets* (St. Paul, Minn.: Catholic Library Service, 1937), p. 128.

[10] Sister M. Claudia Carlen, *op. cit.*, p. 247.

Documents of Pius XII (1939–1949);[11] *Industrialism and the Popes;*[12] and *Catholic Social Principles.*[13]

SOURCES OF QUOTATIONS

All quotations of papal pronouncements are taken from documents that have been translated into the English language in their entirety, or in major part. The pronouncements of Leo XIII and of Pius XI are nearly all taken from the volumes of *Social Wellsprings.*[14] Most quotations of pronouncements by Pius XII are taken from the *Catholic Mind,* or from *The Holy Father Speaks to Newlyweds,* January 3 to October 23, 1940.[15] Quotations are also taken from: *The Pope and the People;*[16] *The Pope Speaks;*[17] *The Unwearied Advocate;*[18] the *Clergy Review; Catholic Action;* the *Tablet* (London); *Catholic Documents* (London);[19] and one quotation is taken from a pamphlet, *Humani Generis.*[20]

Quotations are taken from books and periodicals when possible because they are more easily available in libraries than are pamphlets.

All quotations follow in chronological sequence. After the pronouncement or pronouncements of each pope under a certain category, the name of the pope and the year of the publication of the document are indicated, followed by a semicolon; then the

---

[11] Sister M. Claudia Carlen, I.H.M., *Guide to the Documents of Pius XII* (1939–1949), (Westminster, Md.: The Newman Press, 1951), p. 229.

[12] Mary Lois Eberdt, C.H.M., and Gerald J. Schnepp, S.M., *Industrialism and the Popes* (New York: P. J. Kenedy & Sons, 1953), pp. 192–202.

[13] Cronin, *op. cit.,* pp. 732–734.

[14] Joseph Husslein, S.J. (ed.), *Social Wellsprings* (Milwaukee: The Bruce Publishing Company, 1949).

[15] *The Holy Father Speaks to Newlyweds,* ed. by Edgar Schmiedler, O.S.B., trans. by Bernard Sause, O.S.B., and David Kinish, O.S.B. (Washington, D. C.: The Family Life Bureau, N.C.W.C., 1943), p. 56.

[16] *The Pope and the People* (London: Catholic Truth Society, 1932).

[17] *The Pope Speaks* (New York: Harcourt Brace and Co., 1940).

[18] Vincent A. Yzermans, *The Unwearied Advocate* (Minnesota: St. Cloud, 1954), II, pp. 9–10; 32–33; 35–37.

[19] Published for the Pontifical Court Club by the Salesian Press, Lurrey Lane, Battersea, S.W. 11.

[20] *Humani Generis* (Washington, D. C.: N.C.W.C., 1950).

reference to the quotation is given, with the volume and the page of the publication. The encyclical *Casti Connubii* (CC) of Pius XI, *Social Wellsprings* (*SW*), and the *Catholic Mind* (*CM*) are always abbreviated because they occur frequently. References for quotations used less frequently are given in full.

A chronological list of the papal documents quoted follows the concluding chapter. The list gives the circumstances under which, and to whom, each document was given, followed by references to the original and English texts.

The final supplement consists of a cross reference index.

RELATED LITERATURE, BUT NOT QUOTED

The following papal documents are not public or have not been translated into English.

The encyclical *Constanti Hungarorum,* by Leo XIII, 1893 (September 2), treats of mixed marriages. No complete translation was found in English; an extract was located in *Tablet,* Volume LXXXII (September 9, 1893), pages 409–410.

The encyclical *Quam Religiosa,* by Leo XIII, 1898 (August 16), treats of civil marriage law in Peru. The original text is in *Acta Leonis,* Volume XVIII, pages 140–144; no English text was located.

The encyclical *Dum Multa,* by Leo XIII, 1902 (December 4), deals with marriage in Ecuador. The original text is found in *Acta Leonis,* Volume XXII, pages 260–263; no English text was located.

The most important contribution of Pius X toward marriage is the "Decree Concerning Sponsalia and Matrimony," issued on August 2, 1907, by the Sacred Congregation with the authority of His Holiness.[21] It deals with disciplinary laws governing marriage. It has not been quoted because it is not, strictly speaking, an official document of Pius X himself.

Pius X also outlined woman's social mission; but he always

---

[21] Pius X, "Decree Concerning Sponsalia and Matrimony," *Catholic Mind,* V (July 3, 1907), 332–338.

did this in an address or letter to a Catholic women's organization. In 1904, Pius X wrote to the Daughters of Faith, through the moderator of this society, Elisa O'Brien Lummis, offering encouragement and listing crucial goals for their social apostolate.[22] In December of 1904, Pius X took note of the work of German Catholic women, and wrote to the Baroness de Haxthausen on the religious training of women and young girls.[23] On April 8, 1904, Pius X urged the fight against white slavery and organized vice.[24] On May 20, 1912, Pius X praised women who protected working girls.[25]

In his first public document on woman's position in society, Benedict XV warned against woman becoming the rival of man rather than his co-worker.[26] In the same document, the pope praised Father Augustine Roesler's book, *Die Frauenfrage,* as a guide to Catholic women. Benedict XV addressed a letter to Mother Angela of Our Lady, superior general of the Ursulines, December 27, 1917, in which he denounced secular pursuits of women and the laxity of morals among them and commended the Sisters who train girls to become worthy mothers of families.[27] Women's unions were first mentioned by Benedict XV in a letter on woman's place in economic life to Canon Nury, director of the Catholic Women Workers' Association of the diocese of Autun, France (Letter of Cardinal Gasparri, Documentation Catholique, 1st year, Tome I, May 24, 1919, p. 541).[28] Benedict XV also wrote a letter to Clara Douglas Sherman, onetime president of the International Federation of Catholic Alumnae, in which he extolled modesty in dress.[29]

[22] William B. Faherty, S.J., *The Destiny of Modern Woman* (Westminster, Md.: The Newman Press, 1950), pp. 36, 182, quoting *Acta Sanctae Sedis,* XXXIX (1906), 258–259.

[23] *Ibid.,* pp. 38, 183, quoting *ibid.,* XXIX (1905), 405.

[24] *Ibid.,* pp. 47, 184, quoting *Acta Sanctae Sedis,* XXXIX (1906), 22.

[25] *Ibid.,* pp. 47, 184, quoting *Acta Apostolicae Sedis,* IV (1912), 462.

[26] *Ibid.,* pp. 57, 184, quoting *ibid.,* VII (1915), 7.

[27] *Ibid.,* 57–58, 184, quoting *ibid.,* X (1918), 57; Benedict XV, "Letter Natalis Trecentisimi," *Principles for Peace,* ed. by Rev. Harry C. Koenig (Washington, D. C.: N.C.W.C., 1943), pp. 243–244.

[28] Faherty, *op. cit.,* pp. 62–63, 185.

[29] Benedict XV, "Modesty in Dress," n.d., *Catholic Mind,* XIX (Jan. 22, 1921), 59–60.

Contents

Family Under Communism
Family and Movies
Family Ritual
Rural Family
Urban Family

PAPAL PRONOUNCEMENTS ON MARRIAGE
AND THE FAMILY

Chapter I

Origin and Nature of Marriage

According to traditional Catholic doctrine marriage is a divine institution; it comes directly from God.[1] God created man and woman morally equal but not identical.[2] They are to complement each other physically, emotionally, spiritually, and socially. From the very beginning, marriage was a union between one man and one woman.[3] However, the original form of marriage was gradually lost sight of among the primitive peoples of the world and polygamy made its appearance on the earth. Divorce and moral degradation were the result. When Christ came upon earth He elevated marriage to the status of a sacrament, condemned the Jewish custom of divorce,[4] and committed the discipline and regulation of marriage to the Church.

In this chapter we record quotations from the modern popes restating, emphasizing, or clarifying for modern society the import of this traditional doctrine on the origin and nature of marriage.

ORIGIN OF MARRIAGE

Pope Leo XIII recalls that marriage was instituted in Paradise by God.

. . . We merely record what is known to all and cannot be doubted by any, that God, on the sixth day of creation, after having made man from the slime of the earth, and breathed into

---

[1] Gen. 2:18.
[2] Mk. 10:6.
[3] Gen. 2:23, 24.
[4] Mt. 19:6.

1

his face the breath of life, gave him a companion, miraculously taken by Him from the side of Adam as he was locked in sleep. In His most far-reaching foresight God thus decreed that this husband and wife should be the natural beginning of the human race. From them it might be propagated, and preserved by an unfailing fruitfulness, throughout all futurity of time [Leo XIII, 1880, *Arcanum; SW*, I, 26–27].

Pope Pius XI repeats the traditional Catholic doctrine on the origin of marriage.
. . . Let it be repeated as an immutable and inviolable fundamental doctrine that matrimony was not instituted or restored by man but by God . . . [Pius XI, 1930, CC; *SW*, II, 126].

And Pius XII confirms the teachings of his predecessors when he states:
. . . From the individual and social life we should rise to God, the First Cause and Ultimate Foundation, as He is the Creator of the first conjugal society, from which we have the society which is the family, and the society of peoples and nations [Pius XII, 1942, *Christmas Message, CM*, XLI, 47].

CORRUPTION OF MARRIAGE

Marriage, as it was instituted by God in Paradise, was gradually lost sight of and men changed the institution of marriage to suit their sexual convenience.

THE GENTILES — *Pope Leo XIII reminds us of the corruption and change which overtook marriage among the Gentiles.*
. . . The corruption and change which overtook marriage among the Gentiles seem almost incredible, inasmuch as it was exposed in every land to floods of error and of the most shameful lusts. All nations seem, more or less, to have forgotten the true notion and origin of marriage; and thus everywhere laws were enacted with reference to marriage which were prompted to all appearance by State reasons, but were not such as nature demanded. Solemn rites, invented at the will of the lawgivers,

brought about that women should bear either the honourable name of wife, or as might be, the disgraceful name of concubine. Things, in fact, came to such a pitch that permission to marry, or the refusal of that permission, depended on the will of the heads of the State. . . . Moreover, plurality of wives and husbands, the abounding source of divorces, brought about an exceeding relaxation in the nuptial bond. From the same evil resulted the greatest confusion as to the mutual rights and duties of husbands and wives, inasmuch as a man assumed right of dominion over his wife, ordering her to go about her business, often without any just cause; while he was himself at liberty, as St. Jerome says, "to run headlong with impunity into lust, unbridled and unrestrained, in houses of ill-fame and amongst his female slaves, as if the dignity of the persons sinned with, and not the will of the sinner, made the guilt."

When the licentiousness of a husband thus showed itself, nothing could be more piteous than the fate of the wife, sunk so low as to be all but reckoned a mere means for the gratification of passion, or for the production of offspring. Without any feeling of shame, marriageable girls were bought and sold, just like so much merchandise. Power was sometimes given the father and the husband to inflict capital punishment on the wife. Of necessity the offspring of such marriages as here described were either reckoned among the stock in trade of the commonwealth, or held to be the property of the father of the family. The law in fact permitted him to make and unmake the marriages of his children at his mere will, and even to exercise against them the monstrous power of life and death [Leo XIII, 1880, *Arcanum; SW*, I, 27–28].

THE JEWS — *Pope Leo XIII also states that the Jews lost sight of the original form of marriage and eventually permitted divorce.*

This form of marriage, however, so excellent and so pre-eminent, began to be corrupted by degrees, and to disappear among the heathen; while even among the Jewish race it became clouded in a measure, and obscured. Among them, namely, a common custom had gradually been introduced, by which it was accounted lawful for a man to have more than one wife. And so eventually, when "by reason of the hardness of their heart" (Mt. 19:8), Moses indulgently permitted them to put away their wives, the way was laid open to divorce [Leo XIII, 1880, *Arcanum; SW*, I, 27].

NATURE OF MARRIAGE

The true nature of marriage has been attacked by those who reject the supernatural and also by those who deify the state.

ALL MARRIAGE IS SACRED — *Leo XIII shows that all who deny the sacredness of marriage cannot escape the charge of delusion.*

. . . Marriage has God for its author, and was from the very beginning a kind of foreshadowing of the Incarnation of His Son; and therefore there abides in it a something holy and religious; not extraneous, but innate; not derived from men, but implanted by nature. Innocent III, therefore, and Honorius III, our predecessors, affirmed not falsely nor rashly that a certain sacredness of marriage rites existed ever amongst the faithful and unbelievers. We call to witness the monuments of antiquity, as also the manners and customs of those people who, being the most civilized, had the greatest knowledge of law and equity. In the minds of all of them it was a fixed and foregone conclusion that, when marriage was thought of, it was thought of as conjoined with religion and holiness. Hence among them marriages were commonly celebrated with religious ceremonies, under the authority of pontiffs, and with the ministry of priests. So mighty, even in the souls ignorant of heavenly doctrine, was the force of nature, of the remembrance of their origin, and of the conscience of the human race [Leo XIII, 1880, *Arcanum; SW*, I, 33].

The sacredness of marriage is evident, says Pius XI.

. . . This sacredness of marriage which is intimately connected with religion and all that is holy, arises from the divine origin . . . , from its purpose which is the begetting and educating of children for God, and the binding of man and wife to God through Christian love and mutual support; and finally it arises from the very nature of wedlock, whose institution is to be sought for in the far-seeing providence of God, whereby it is the means of transmitting life, thus making the parents the ministers, as it were, of the Divine Omnipotence. To this must be added that new element of dignity which comes from the sacrament, by which the Christian marriage is so ennobled and raised to such a level, that it appeared to the Apostle as a great mystery, honorable in every way (Eph. 5:32; Hebr. 13:4) [Pius XI, 1930, CC; *SW*, II, 153].

FREE CONSENT ESSENTIAL — *Pius XI points out the fact that free consent on the part of each of the spouses is absolutely necessary to constitute a true marriage.*

Yet although matrimony is of its very nature of divine institution, the human will, too, enters into it and performs a most noble part. For each individual marriage, inasmuch as it is a conjugal union of a particular man and woman, arises only from the free consent of each of the spouses; and this free act of the will, by which each party hands over and accepts those rights proper to the state of marriage, is so necessary to constitute true marriage that it cannot be supplied by any human power (*Cod. jur. can.*, c. 1081, 1, 2). This freedom, however, regards only the question whether the contracting parties really wish to enter upon matrimony or to marry this particular person. The nature itself of matrimony is entirely independent of the free will of man, so that once a person has contracted matrimony he is thereby subject to its divinely made laws and its essential properties. For the Angelic Doctor, writing on conjugal honor and on offspring as the fruit of marriage, says: "These things are so contained in matrimony by the marriage pact itself that, if anything to the contrary were expressed in the consent which makes the marriage, it would not be a true marriage."

By matrimony, therefore, the souls of the contracting parties are joined and knit together more directly and more intimately than are their bodies, and that not by any passing affection of sense or spirit, but by a deliberate and firm act of the will; and from this union of souls by God's decree, a sacred and inviolable bond arises.

Hence the nature of this contract, which is proper and peculiar to it alone, makes it entirely different both from the union of animals entered into by the blind instinct of nature alone, in which neither reason nor free will plays a part, and also from the haphazard unions of men, which are far removed from all true and honorable unions of will and enjoy none of the rights of family life.

*　　*　　*

Therefore the sacred partnership of true marriage is constituted both by the will of God and the will of man. From God comes the very institution of marriage, the ends for which it was instituted, the laws that govern it, the blessings that flow from it; while man, through generous surrender of his own person made to another for the whole span of life, becomes, with the help and co-operation of God, the author of each particular marriage, with the duties and blessings annexed thereto from divine institution [Pius XI, 1930, CC; *SW*, II, 126–128].

MARRIAGE OF NONBAPTIZED IS A CONTRACT — *In drawing a distinction between Christian marriages and other marriages, Pope Leo XIII states that "marriage is the contract itself, whenever that contract is lawfully concluded" (Leo XIII, 1880,* Arcanum; SW, *I, 35*).

Pius XII reaffirms the teaching of Leo XIII when he writes: . . . Because the Creator has willed it to be, marriage is a res sacra, a sacred thing. . . . Where the parties are not baptized, marriage legitimately contracted is a sacred thing in the natural order [Pius XII, 1946, *On Faith and Marriage; CM*, XLV, 133].

IN CHRISTIAN MARRIAGE THE CONTRACT IS A SACRAMENT — *Leo XIII denounces the court legists who insist on severing the matrimonial contract from the sacrament in Christian marriages.*

. . . For certain it is that in Christian marriage the contract is inseparable from the sacrament; and that for this reason, the contract cannot be true and legitimate without being a sacrament as well. For Christ our Lord added to marriage the dignity of a sacrament.

* * *

Marriage, moreover, is a sacrament, because it is a holy sign which gives grace, showing forth an image of the mystical nuptials of Christ with the Church. But the form and image of these nuptials is shown precisely by the very bond of that most close union in which man and woman are bound together in one; which bond is nothing else but the marriage itself. Hence it is clear that among Christians every true marriage is, in itself and by itself, a sacrament; and nothing can be further from the truth than to say that the sacrament is a certain added ornament, or outward endowment, which can be separated and torn away from the contract at the caprice of man [Leo XIII, 1880, *Arcanum;* *SW,* I, 35–36].

When speaking about the dignity of Christian marriage, Leo XIII says:

. . . To the Apostles, indeed, as our masters, are to be referred the doctrines which "our holy Fathers, the Councils, and the Tradition of the Universal Church have always taught" (Trid. Sess. xxiv in pr.), namely — that Christ our Lord raised marriage to the dignity of a sacrament; that to husband and wife, guarded and strengthened by the heavenly grace which His merits gained for them, He gave power to attain holiness in the married state; and that, in a wondrous way, making marriage an example of the mystical union between Himself and His Church, He not only perfected that love which is according to nature, but also made the natural union of one man with one woman far more perfect through the bond of heavenly love. Paul says to the Ephesians: ". . . This is a great sacrament; but I speak in Christ and in the church" (5:25–32) [Leo XIII, 1880, *Arcanum; SW,* I, 29].

In his first encyclical, Leo XIII writes the following about marriage:

. . . Elevating to the dignity of a sacrament the ceremony of marriage, Jesus Christ wished to make of it a symbol of His union with the Church, and thereby has not only rendered more holy the conjugal union, but has prepared for the parents as well as for the children the most efficacious aids to achieve more readily the accomplishment of their mutual duties and attain to the possession of temporal and eternal felicity [Leo XIII, 1878, *Inscrutabili; SW*, I, 10].

Leo XIII mentions the harmful doctrines of Socialism, and then writes:

. . . But the Church, on the contrary, teaches that "marriage, honorable in all" (Hebr. 13), which God Himself instituted in the very beginning of the world and made indissoluble for the propagation and preservation of the human species, has become still more binding and more holy through Christ, who raised it to the dignity of a sacrament, and chose to use it as the figure of His own union with the Church [Leo XIII, 1878, *Quod Apostolici Muneris; SW*, I, 20].

Writing on the dignity of Christian wedlock in the first paragraph of his encyclical on Christian Marriage, *Pope Pius XI states:*

. . . Christ our Lord, Son of the Eternal Father, having assumed the nature of fallen man, and burning with His loving desire of compassing the redemption of our race, not only ordained it in an especial manner as the principle and foundation of domestic society and therefore of all human intercourse, but also raised it to the rank of a truly "great" sacrament of the New Law . . . [Pius XI, 1930, CC; *SW*, II, 125].

Concerning the sacramental grace of matrimony, Pius XI writes:

But considering the benefits of the sacrament, besides the firmness and indissolubility, there are also much higher emoluments as the word "sacrament" itself very aptly indicates; for to Christians this is not a meaningless and empty name. Christ the Lord, the Institutor and "Perfector" of the holy sacraments, by raising the matrimony of His faithful to the dignity of a true sacrament of the New Law, made it a sign and source of that peculiar internal grace by which "it perfects natural love, it confirms an indissoluble union, and sanctifies both man and wife" (Conc. Trid., Sess. xxiv).

And since the valid matrimonial consent among the faithful was constituted by Christ as a sign of grace, the sacramental nature is so intimately bound up with Christian wedlock that there can be no true marriage between baptized persons "without being by that very fact a sacrament" (*Cod. jur. can.*, c. 1012).

By the very fact, therefore, that the faithful with sincere mind give such consent, they open up for themselves a treasure of sacramental grace from which they draw supernatural power for the fulfilling of their rights and duties faithfully, holily, perseveringly even unto death.

Hence this sacrament not only increases sanctifying grace, the permanent principle of the supernatural life, in those who, as the expression is, place no obstacle (obex) in its way, but also adds particular gifts, dispositions, seeds of grace, by elevating and perfecting the natural powers. By these gifts the parties are assisted not only in understanding, but in knowing intimately, in adhering to firmly, in willing effectively, and in successfully putting into practice, those things which pertain to the marriage state, its aims and duties, and giving them in fine right to the actual assistance of grace, whensoever they need it for fulfillment of the duties of their state.

Nevertheless, since it is a law of divine providence in the supernatural order that men do not reap the full fruit of the sacraments which they receive after acquiring the use of reason unless they co-operate with grace, the grace of matrimony will remain for the most part an unused talent hidden in the field unless the parties exercise these supernatural powers and cultivate and develop the seeds of grace they have received. If, how-

ever, doing all that lies within their power, they co-operate diligently, they will be able with ease to bear the burdens of their
state and to fulfill their duties. By such a sacrament they will
be strengthened, sanctified, and in a manner consecrated. For, as
St. Augustine teaches, just as by Baptism and Holy Orders a
man is set aside and assisted either for the duties of Christian
life or for the priestly office and is never deprived of their
sacramental aid, almost in the same way (although not by a sacramental character), the faithful once joined by marriage ties
can never be deprived of the help and the binding force of the
sacrament.

*　　　*　　　*

. . . Let them constantly keep in mind, that they have been
sanctified and strengthened for the duties and for the dignity of
their state by a special sacrament, the efficacious power of which,
although it does not impress a character, is undying. To this purpose we may ponder over the words full of real comfort of holy
Cardinal Robert Bellarmine, who with other well-known theologians with devout conviction thus expresses himself: "The sacrament of matrimony can be regarded in two ways: first, in the
making, and then in its permanent state. For it is a sacrament
like to that of the Eucharist, which not only when it is being
conferred, but also whilst it remains, is a sacrament; for as long
as the married parties are alive, so long is their union a sacrament
of Christ and the Church" [Pius XI, 1930, CC; *SW*, II, 138–140,
165–166].

To newlyweds, Pius XII said:
. . . The sacrament makes of marriage itself a means of mutual
sanctification for the married and a source of inexhaustible supernatural helps; makes of their union a symbol of that between
Christ and His Church; makes them collaborators with the
Father in His creative works, with the Son in His redeeming
work, with the Holy Ghost in His work of illumination and education . . . [Pius XII, 1940, *Scritti e Discorsi*, II; *The Holy
Father Speaks to Newlyweds*, p. 30].

Addressing the National Congress of the "Family Front" and the Association of Large Families, November 26, 1951, His Holiness, Pius XII, said:

In the natural order, among social institutions, there is none which the Church has closer to her heart than the family. Marriage, which is its root, was raised by Christ to the dignity of a sacrament . . . [Pius XII, 1952, *Morality in Marriage; CM, L*, 307].

UNITY

The institution of marriage is a definite creation of God, and it was from the beginning a union for life between one man and one woman only.

To prove the doctrine on the unity of marriage, Leo XIII writes:

. . . From the Gospel we see clearly that this doctrine was declared and openly confirmed by the divine authority of Jesus Christ. He bore witness to the Jews and to His Apostles that marriage, from its institution, should exist between two only, namely, between one man and one woman; that of two they are made, so to say, one flesh; and that the marriage bond is by the will of God so closely and strongly made fast that no man may dissolve it or rend it asunder. "For this cause shall a man leave father and mother, and shall cleave to his wife, and they two shall be in one flesh. Therefore now they are not two, but one flesh. What, therefore, God hath joined together, let no man put asunder" (Mt. 19:5, 6) [Leo XIII, 1880, *Arcanum; SW*, I, 27].

On the unity of marriage, Pius XI writes:

Wherefore, conjugal faith, or honor, demands in the first place the complete unity of matrimony which the Creator Himself laid down in the beginning when He wished it to be not otherwise than between one man and one woman. And although afterward this primeval law was relaxed to some extent by God, the Supreme Legislator, there is no doubt that the law of the Gospel fully restored that original and perfect unity, and abrogated all dispensations as the words of Christ and the constant teaching and action of the Church show plainly. With reason, therefore, does the Sacred Council of Trent solemnly declare: "Christ our Lord very clearly taught that in this bond two persons only are to be united and joined together when He said: 'Therefore they are no longer two, but one flesh'" (Conc. Trid., Sess. xxiv) [Pius XI, 1930, CC; *SW*, II, 132].

INDISSOLUBILITY

Leo XIII stresses the indissolubility of marriage when he writes:
. . . In like manner from the teaching of the Apostles we learn that the unity of marriage and its perpetual indissolubility, the indispensable conditions of its very origin, must, according to the command of Christ, be holy and inviolable without exception. Paul says again: "To them that are married, not I, but the Lord commandeth that the wife depart not from her husband; and if she depart, that she remain unmarried or be reconciled to her husband" (1 Cor. 7:10, 11). And again: "A woman is bound by the law as long as her husband liveth; but if her husband die, she is at liberty" (*ibid.*, 39).

*   *   *

. . . It should further be known that no power can dissolve the bond of Christian marriage whenever this has been ratified and consummated; and that, as a consequence, those husbands and wives are guilty of a manifest crime who plan, for whatsoever reason, to be united in a second marriage before the first one has been ended by death . . . [Leo XIII, 1880, *Arcanum; SW*, I, 29, 44].

That indissolubility is essential to marriage is evident from the words of Pius XI:
. . . This is the doctrine of Holy Scripture (Gen. 1:27–28; 2:22–23; Mt. 19:3 ff.; Eph. 5:33 ff.); this is the constant tradition of the Universal Church; this is the solemn definition of the Sacred Council of Trent, which declares and establishes from the words of Holy Writ itself that God is the Author of the

perpetual stability of the marriage bond, its unity and its firmness (Conc. Trid., Sess. xxiv).

*   *   *

In the first place Christ Himself lays stress on the indissolubility and firmness of the marriage bond when He says: "What therefore God has joined, let no man put asunder" (Mt. 19:6), and: "Everyone that putteth away his wife and marrieth another committeth adultery, and he that marrieth her that is put away from her husband committeth adultery" (Lk. 16:18).

And St. Augustine clearly places what he calls the blessing of matrimony in this indissolubility when he says: "In the sacrament it is provided that the marriage bond should not be broken, and that a husband or wife, if separated, should not be joined to another even for the sake of offspring."

And this inviolable stability, although not in the same perfect measure in every case, belongs to every true marriage, for the word of the Lord: "What God hath joined together let no man put asunder," must of necessity include all true marriages without exception, since it was spoken of the marriage of our first parents, the prototype of every future marriage. Therefore although before Christ the sublimeness and the severity of the primeval law was so tempered that Moses permitted to the chosen people of God on account of the hardness of their hearts that a bill of divorce might be given in certain circumstances, nevertheless, Christ, by virtue of His supreme legislative power, recalled this concession of greater liberty and restored the primeval law in its integrity by those words which must never be forgotten, "What therefore God has joined, let no man put asunder." Wherefore, Our predecessor, Pius VI, of happy memory, writing to the bishop of Agria, most wisely said: "Hence it is clear that marriage even in the state of nature, and certainly long before it was raised to the dignity of a sacrament, was divinely instituted in such a way that it should carry with it a perpetual and indissoluble bond which cannot therefore be dissolved by any civil law. Therefore although the sacramental element may be absent from a marriage as is the case among unbelievers, still in such a marriage, inasmuch as it is a true marriage there must remain and indeed there does remain that perpetual bond which by divine right is so bound up with matrimony from its first institution that it is not subject to any civil power. And so, whatever marriage is said to be contracted, either it is so contracted that it is really a true marriage, in which case it carries with it that enduring bond which by divine right is inherent in every true marriage; or it is thought to be contracted without that perpetual bond, and in that case there is no marriage, but an illicit union opposed of its very nature to the divine law, which therefore cannot be entered into or maintained" (July 11, 1789).

And if this stability seems to be open to exception, however rare the exception may be, as in the case of certain natural marriages between unbelievers, or among Christians in the case of those marriages which though valid have not been consummated, that exception does not depend on the will of men nor on that of any merely human power, but on divine law, of which the only guardian and interpreter is the Church of Christ. However, not even this power can ever affect for any cause whatsoever a Christian marriage which is valid and has been consummated, for as it is plain that here the marriage contract has its full completion, so, by the will of God, there is also the greatest firmness and indissolubility which may not be destroyed by any human authority.

If we wish with all reverence to inquire into the intimate reason of this divine decree, Venerable Brethren, we shall easily see it in the mystical signification of Christian marriage which is fully and perfectly verified in consummated marriage between Christians. For, as the Apostle says in his Epistle to the Ephesians, the marriage of Christians recalls that most perfect union which exists between Christ and the Church: Sacramentum hoc magnum est, ego autem dico, in Christo et in Ecclesia, "This is a great sacrament; but I say, in Christ and in the church" (Eph. 5:32), which union, as long as Christ shall live and the Church through Him, can never be dissolved by any separation . . .

[Pius XI, 1930, CC; *SW*, II, 126, 135–137].

To stress the indissolubility of marriage, Pius XII says:
. . . The farthest limit of her power [the Church's] is solemnly formulated in Canon 1118 of the Code of Canon Law: Valid marriage ratified and consummated can be dissolved by no human power and by no other cause but death [Pius XII, 1946, *On Faith and Marriage; CM,* XLV, 134].

BENEFITS OF STABILITY

Pope Pius XI enumerates the benefits which flow from the indissolubility of Christian marriage. He writes:
Indeed, how many and how important are the benefits which flow from the indissolubility of matrimony cannot escape anyone who gives even a brief consideration either to the good of the married parties and the offspring or to the welfare of human society. First of all, both husband and wife possess a positive guarantee of the endurance of this stability which that generous yielding of their persons and the intimate fellowship of their hearts by their nature strongly require, since true love never falls away (1 Cor. 13:8). Besides, a strong bulwark is set up in defense of a loyal chastity against incitements to infidelity, should any be encountered either from within or from without. Any anxious fear lest in adversity or old age the other spouse would prove unfaithful is precluded and in its place there reigns a calm sense of security. Moreover, the dignity of both man and wife is maintained and mutual aid is most satisfactorily assured, while through the indissoluble bond, always enduring, the spouses are warned continuously that not for the sake of perishable things nor that they may serve their passions, but that they may procure one for the other high and lasting good have they entered into the nuptial partnership, to be dissolved only by death. In the training and education of children, which must extend over a period of many years, it plays a great part, since the grave and long enduring burdens of this office are best borne by the united efforts of the parents. Nor do lesser benefits accrue

to human society as a whole. For experience has taught that un-assailable stability in matrimony is a fruitful source of virtuous life and of habits of integrity. Where this order of things obtains, the happiness and well-being of the nation is safely guarded; what the families and individuals are, that also is the state, for a body is determined by its parts. Wherefore, both for the private good of husband, wife, and children, as likewise for the public good of human society, they indeed deserve well who strenuously defend the inviolable stability of matrimony [Pius XI, 1930, CC; *SW*, II, 137–138].

CONJUGAL FIDELITY

Since marriage is a contract between one man and one woman, it follows that by marriage husband and wife pledge to give to each other what they cannot give to any third party. Therefore, Leo XIII writes:

. . . Husband and wife . . . are bound, namely, to have such feelings for one another as to cherish always very great mutual love, to be ever faithful to their marriage vow . . . [Leo XIII, 1880, *Arcanum; SW*, I, 30].

And Pius XI states:

. . . The Holy Doctor (St. Augustine) himself expressly de-clares . . . : "By conjugal faith it is provided that there should be no carnal intercourse outside the marriage bond with another man or woman. . . ."

*　　　*　　　*

The second blessing of matrimony which We said was men-tioned by St. Augustine, is the blessing of conjugal honor which consists in the mutual fidelity of the spouses in fulfilling the marriage contract, so that what belongs to one of the parties by reason of this contract sanctioned by divine law, may not be denied to him or permitted to any third person. Nor may any-thing be conceded to one of the parties which is contrary to the rights and laws of God and entirely opposed to matrimonial faith, and so can never be conceded.

*　*　*

Nay, that mutual familiar intercourse between the spouses themselves, if the blessing of conjugal faith is to shine with becoming splendor, must be distinguished by chastity so that husband and wife conform themselves in all things to the law of God and of nature, and endeavor always to follow the will of their most wise and holy Creator with the greatest reverence toward the work of God.

This conjugal faith, however, which is most aptly called by St. Augustine the "faith of chastity" blooms more freely, more beautifully and more nobly, when it is rooted in that more excellent soil, the love of husband and wife which pervades all the duties of married life and holds pride of place in Christian marriage. For matrimonial faith demands that husband and wife be joined in an especially holy and pure love, not as adulterers love each other, but as Christ loved the Church. This precept the Apostle laid down when he said: "Husbands, love your wives just as Christ also loved the Church" (Eph. 5:25; Col. 3:19), that Church which of a truth He embraced with a boundless love not for the sake of His own advantage, but seeking only the good of His Spouse.

The love, then, of which We are speaking is not that based on the passing lust of the moment nor does it consist in pleasing words only, but in the deep attachment of the heart which is expressed in action, since love is proved by deeds. This outward expression of love in the home demands not only mutual help but must go further; must have as its primary purpose that man and wife help each other day by day in forming and perfecting themselves in the interior life, so that through their partnership in life they may advance ever more and more in virtue, and above all that they may grow in true love toward God and their neighbor, on which indeed "depend the whole Law and the Prophets" (Mt. 22:40).

*　*　*

This mutual interior molding of husband and wife, this determined effort to perfect each other, can in a very real sense, as the Roman Catechism teaches, be said to be the chief reason and purpose of matrimony, provided matrimony be looked at not in the restricted sense, as instituted for the proper conception and education of the child, but more widely, as the blending of life as a whole and the mutual interchange and sharing thereof.

By this same love it is necessary that all the other rights and duties of the marriage state be regulated so that the words of the Apostle: "Let the husband render to the wife her due, and likewise the wife to the husband" (1 Cor. 7:3), express not only a law of justice but of charity [Pius XI, 1930, CC; *SW*, II, 129, 131–133].

His Holiness, Pius XII, instructed newlyweds as follows:

Conjugal fidelity is your gold, or rather, a treasure to be preferred to all the gold in the world. The sacrament of matrimony gives you the means of possessing and augmenting this treasure. Offer it to God that He may help you to preserve it better. Gold because of its beauty, its brilliance, its unalterableness, is the most precious of metals; its value is the base and measure of other riches. So also conjugal fidelity is the base and measure of all domestic happiness. Every part of the temple of Solomon was covered with gold (3 Kings 6:22) to preserve the materials as well as to beautify the whole. Similarly the gold of fidelity, to assure the constancy and the luster of the conjugal union, should clothe and envelop it completely. Gold, to preserve its beauty and luster, must be pure. In like manner the fidelity of husband and wife must be complete and unsullied. If it begins to deteriorate, there is an end to confidence, peace, and happiness [Pius XII, 1940, *Scritti e Discorsi*, II; *The Holy Father Speaks to Newlyweds*, p. 7].

ADULTERY

Marriage does not entitle anyone to love affairs with a third party. A friendship of a sensual nature that even goes so far as sexual intimacies is indeed sinful. Concerning adultery, Pope Pius XI has this to say:

Nor did Christ our Lord wish only to condemn any form of polygamy or polyandry, as they are called, whether successive or simultaneous, and every other external dishonorable act, but, in order that the sacred bonds of marriage may be guarded absolutely inviolate, He forbade also even wilful thoughts and desires of such like things: "But I say to you, that anyone who even looks with lust at a woman has already committed adultery with her in his heart" (Mt. 5:28). Which words of Christ our Lord cannot be annulled even by the consent of one of the partners of marriage for they express a law of God and of nature which no will of man can break or bend.

* * *

. . . St. Augustine clearly declares in these words: . . . that when for the sake of begetting children, women marry or are taken to wife, it is wrong to leave a wife that is sterile in order to take another by whom children may be had. Anyone doing this is guilty of adultery.

* * *

It follows therefore that they are destroying mutual fidelity, who think that the ideas and morality of our present time concerning a certain harmful and false friendship with a third party can be countenanced, and who teach that a greater freedom of feeling and action in such external relations should be allowed to man and wife, particularly as many (so they consider) are possessed of an inborn sexual tendency which cannot be satisfied within the narrow limits of monogamous marriage. That rigid attitude which condemns all sensual affections and actions with a third party they imagine to be a narrowing of mind and heart, something obsolete, or an abject form of jealousy, and as a result they look upon whatever penal laws are passed by the state for the preserving of conjugal faith as void or to be abolished.

Such unworthy and idle opinions are condemned by that noble instinct which is found in every chaste husband and wife, and even by the light of the testimony of nature alone — a testimony that is sanctioned and confirmed by the command of God: "Thou shalt not commit adultery" (Exod. 20:14), and the words of Christ: "Anyone who even looks with lust at a woman has already committed adultery with her in his heart" (Mt. 5:28). The force of this divine precept can never be weakened by any merely human custom, bad example or pretext of human progress, for just as the one "Jesus Christ is the same yesterday and to-day, yes, and forever" (Hebr. 13:8), so it is the one and the same doctrine of Christ that abides and of which not one jot or tittle shall pass away till all things have been accomplished (Mt. 5:18) [Pius XI, 1930, CC; *SW*, II, 132, 137, 149–150].

THE POSITION AND THE RELATION OF HUSBAND AND WIFE IN THE FAMILY

More than once did Leo XIII refer to the mutual life of husband and wife. He wrote:

Wherefore, as the apostle has it (Eph. 5), as Christ is the head of the Church, so is the man the head of the woman; and as the Church is subject to Christ, who embraces her with a most chaste and undying love, so also should wives be subject to their husbands, and be loved by them in turn with a faithful and constant affection . . . [Leo XIII, 1878, *Quod Apostolici Muneris; SW*, I, 20].

. . . The husband is the chief of the family, and the head of the wife. The woman, because she is flesh of his flesh, and bone of his bone, must be subject to her husband and obey him; not, indeed, as a servant, but as a companion, so that her obedience shall be wanting in neither honour nor dignity. Since the husband represents Christ, and since the wife represents the Church, let there always be, both in him who commands and in her who obeys, a heaven-born love guiding both in their respective duties. For "the husband is the head of the wife; as Christ is the head of the church. . . . Therefore, as the church is subject to Christ, so also let wives be to their husbands in all things" (Eph. 5:23, 24).

*   *   *

. . . A law of marriage just to all, and the same for all, was enacted by the abolition of the old distinction between slaves and free-born men and women; and thus rights of husbands and wives were made equal: for, as St. Jerome says, "with us that which is unlawful for women is unlawful for men also, and the same restraint is imposed on equal conditions." The selfsame rights also were firmly established for reciprocal affection and for the interchange of duties; the dignity of the woman was asserted and assured; and it was forbidden to the man to inflict capital punishment for adultery, or lustfully and shamelessly to violate his plighted faith [Leo XIII, 1880, *Arcanum; SW*, I, 30–31].

Speaking about the domestic society, Pope Pius XI states:

. . . There should flourish in it that "order of love," as St. Augustine calls it. This order includes both the primacy of the husband with regard to the wife and children, and the ready subjection of the wife and her willing obedience, which the Apostle commends in these words: "Let women be subject to their husbands as to the Lord, because the husband is the head of the wife, as Christ is the head of the Church" (Eph. 5:22–23).

This subjection, however, does not deny or take away the liberty which fully belongs to the woman both in view of her dignity as a human person, and in view of her most noble office as wife and mother and companion; nor does it bid her obey her husband's every request if not in harmony with right reason or with the dignity due to the wife; nor, in fine, does it imply that the wife should be put on a level with those persons who in law are called minors, to whom it is not customary to allow free exercise of their rights on account of their lack of mature judgment, or of their ignorance of human affairs. But it forbids that exaggerated liberty which cares not for the good of the family; it forbids that in this body which is the family, the heart be separated from the head to the great detriment of the whole body and the proximate danger of ruin. For if the man is the head, the woman is the heart, and as he occupies the chief place in ruling, so she may and ought to claim for herself the chief place in love.

Again, this subjection of wife to husband in its degree and manner may vary according to the different conditions of persons, place, and time. In fact, if the husband neglect his duty, it falls to the wife to take his place in directing the family. But the structure of the family and its fundamental law, established and confirmed by God, must always and everywhere be maintained intact.

*   *   *

This equality of rights which is so much exaggerated and distorted must indeed be recognized in those rights which belong to the dignity of the human soul and which are proper to the marriage contract and inseparably bound up with wedlock. In such things undoubtedly both parties enjoy the same rights and are bound by the same obligations; in other things there must be a certain inequality and due accommodation, which is demanded by the good of the family and the right ordering and unity and stability of home life [Pius XI, 1930, CC; *SW*, II, 133–134, 151].

Speaking about the characteristics of the two sexes and their mutual co-ordination, Pius XII writes:

In their personal dignity as children of God a man and woman are absolutely equal, as they are in relation to the last end of human life, which is everlasting union with God in the happiness of heaven. It is the undying glory of the Church that she put these truths in their proper light and honorable place and that she has freed woman from degrading, unnatural slavery.

But a man and woman cannot maintain and perfect this equal dignity of theirs, unless by respecting and activating characteristic qualities which nature has given each of them, physical and spiritual qualities which cannot be eliminated, which cannot be reversed without nature itself stepping in to restore the balance. These characteristic qualities which divide the two sexes are so obvious to all that only willful blindness or a no less disastrous utopian doctrinaire attitude could overlook or practically ignore their significance in social relations.

The two sexes, by the very qualities that distinguish them, are mutually complementary to such an extent that their co-ordination makes itself felt in every phase of man's social life . . . [Pius XII, 1945, *Woman's Duties in Social and Political Life; CM,* XLIII, 706].

THE CHURCH AND MARRIAGE

Leo XIII strongly defends the Church's authority over Christian marriages.

. . . The Church, always and everywhere, has so used her power with reference to the marriages of Christians, that men have seen clearly how it belongs to her as of native right; not being made hers by any human grant, but given divinely to her by the will of her Founder. Her constant and watchful care in guarding marriage, by the preservation of its sanctity, is so well understood as not to need proof. That the judgment of the Council of Jerusalem reprobated licentious and free love (Acts 15:29), we all know; as also that the incestuous Corinthian was condemned by the authority of blessed Paul (1 Cor. 5:5). Again, in the very beginning of the Christian Church were repulsed and defeated, with the like unremitting determination, the efforts of many who aimed at the destruction of Christian marriage, such as the Gnostics, Manichaeans, and Montanists; and in our own time Mormons, St. Simonians, Phalansterians, and Communists.

*   *   *

. . . It is plainly proved that the legislative and judicial authority of which We are speaking has been freely and constantly used by the Church, even in times when some foolishly suppose the head of the State either to have consented to it or connived at it. It would, for instance, be incredible and altogether absurd to assume that Christ our Lord condemned the long-standing practice of polygamy and divorce by authority delegated to Him by the procurator of the province, or the principal ruler of the Jews. And it would be equally extravagant to think that, when the Apostle Paul taught that divorces and incestuous marriages were not lawful, it was because Tiberius, Caligula, and Nero agreed with him or secretly commanded him so to teach. No man in his senses could ever be persuaded that the Church made so many laws about the holiness and indissolubility of marriage, and the marriages of slaves with the free-born, doing all this by the power received from Roman Emperors most hostile to the Christian name, whose strongest desire was to destroy by violence and murder the rising Church of Christ. Still less could any one believe this to be the case, when the law of the Church was sometimes so divergent from the civil law that Ignatius the Martyr, Justin, Athanagoras, and Tertullian publicly denounced as unjust and adulterous certain marriages which had been sanctioned by Imperial law.

Furthermore, after all power had devolved upon the Christian Emperors, the Supreme Pontiffs and Bishops assembled in Council persisted, with the same independence and consciousness of their right, in commanding or forbidding in regard to marriage whatever they judged to be profitable or expedient for the time being, however much it might seem to be at variance with the laws of the State. It is well known that, with respect to the impediments arising from the marriage bond, through vow, disparity of worship, blood relationship, certain forms of crime, and from previously plighted troth, many decrees were issued by the rulers of the Church in the Councils of Illiberis, Arles, Chalcedon, the second of Milevum, and others, which were often widely different from the decrees sanctioned by the laws of the Empire. Furthermore, so far were Christian princes from arrogating any power in the matter of Christian marriage, that they on the contrary acknowledged and declared that it belonged exclusively in all its fullness to the Church. In fact, Honorius, the younger Theodosius, and Justinian also, hesitated not to confess that the only power belonging to them in relation to marriage was that of acting as guardians and defenders of the Holy Canons. If at any time they enacted anything by their edicts concerning impediments of marriage, they voluntarily explained the reason, affirming that they took it upon themselves so to act, by leave and authority of the Church, whose judgment they were wont to appeal to and reverently to accept, in all questions that concerned legitimacy and divorce; as also in all those points which in any way have a necessary connexion with the marriage bond. The Council of Trent, therefore, had the clearest right to define that it is in the Church's power "to establish diriment impediments of matrimony," and that "matrimonial causes pertain to ecclesiastical judges" (Sess. xxiv, can. 4, 12) [Leo XIII, 1880, *Arcanum; SW*, I, 31, 34–35].

Pope Leo XIII maintains that marriage falls under the authority of the Church because marriage is sacred.

. . . The dignity of the sacrament must be considered; for through addition of the sacrament the marriages of Christians have become far the noblest of all matrimonial unions. But to decree and ordain concerning the sacrament is, by the will of Christ Himself, so much a part of the power and duty of the Church, that it is plainly absurd to maintain that even the very smallest fraction of such power has been transferred to the civil ruler.

* * *

. . . Since marriage, then, is holy by its own power, in its own nature, and of itself, it ought not to be regulated and administered by the will of civil rulers, but by the divine authority of the Church, which alone in sacred matters professes the office of teaching.

* * *

. . . Neither, therefore, by reasoning can it be shown, nor by any testimony of history be proved, that power over the marriages of Christians has ever lawfully been handed over to the rulers of the State . . . [Leo XIII, 1880, *Arcanum; SW*, 1, 33–36].

The Church is the defender of marriage and the human race, states Leo XIII.

It cannot then be denied that the Church has deserved exceedingly well of all nations by her ever watchful care in guarding the sanctity and the indissolubility of marriage. And so, too, no small amount of gratitude is due her for having openly denounced during the last hundred years the wicked laws which grievously offended on this particular point, no less than for having branded with her anathema the baneful heresy obtaining among Protestants regarding divorce and separation. To this must be added her deserts for having in many ways condemned the habitual dissolution of marriage among the Greeks; for having declared invalid all marriages contracted upon the understanding that they may be at some future time dissolved; and lastly, for having, from the earliest times, repudiated the imperial laws which disastrously favoured divorce.

As often, indeed, as the Supreme Pontiffs have resisted the threatening demands of the most powerful amongst rulers that divorces carried out by them should be confirmed by the Church, so often must we account them to have been contending for the safety, not only of religion, but also of the human race. For this reason all generations of men will admire the proofs of unbending courage which are to be found in the decrees of Nicholas I against Lothair; of Urban II and Paschal II against Philip I of France; of Celestine III and Innocent III against Alphonsus of Leon and Philip II of France; of Clement VII and Paul III against Henry VIII; and lastly, of Pius VII, that holy and courageous Pontiff, against Napoleon I, when at the height of his prosperity and in the fulness of his power.

*   *   *

It is also a great blessing that the Church has limited, so far as is needful, the power of fathers of families, so that sons and daughters, wishing to marry, are not in any way deprived of their rightful freedom; that, for the purpose of spreading more widely the supernatural love of husbands and wives, she has decreed marriages within certain degrees of consanguinity or affinity to be null and void; that she has taken the greatest pains to safeguard marriage, as much as is possible, from error and violence and deceit; that she has always wished to preserve the holy chasteness of the marriage-bed, personal rights, the honour of husband and wife, and the security of religion.

Lastly, with such power and with such foresight of legislation has the Church guarded this divine institution, that no one who thinks rightfully of these matters can fail to see how, with regard to marriage, she is the best guardian and defender of the human race; and how withal her wisdom has come forth victorious from the lapse of years, from the assaults of men, and from the countless changes of public events [Leo XIII, 1880, *Arcanum;* *SW*, I, 41, 31–32].

Leo XIII asks civic powers to co-operate with the Church in matters pertaining to marriage.

. . . All rulers and administrators of the State who are desirous of following the dictates of reason and wisdom, and anxious for the good of their people, ought to resolve that they will keep intact the holy laws of marriage; and will make use of the proffered aid of the Church for securing the safety of morals and the happiness of families, rather than suspect her of hostile intention, and falsely and wickedly accuse her of violating the civil law.

They should do this the more readily because the Catholic Church, though powerless in any way to abandon the duties of her office or the defence of her authority, still very greatly inclines to kindness and indulgence whenever these are consistent with the safety of her rights and the sanctity of her duties. Wherefore she makes no decrees in relation to marriage without having regard to the state of the body politic and the condition of the general public; and has besides more than once mitigated, as far as possible, the enactments of her own laws, when there were just and weighty reasons. Moreover she is not unaware, and never calls in doubt, that the sacrament of marriage, since it was instituted for the preservation and increase of the human race, has a necessary relation to various circumstances of life, which, though connected with marriage, belong to the civil order, and about which the State rightly makes strict enquiry and justly promulgates decrees.

Yet no one doubts that Jesus Christ, the Founder of the

Church, willed her sacred power to be distinct from the civil power, and each power to be free and unshackled in its own sphere: with this condition, however, — a condition good alike for both, and of advantage to all men — that union and concord should be maintained between them; and that in such questions as are, though in different ways, of common right and authority, the power to which secular matters have been entrusted should happily and becomingly depend on the other power which has in its charge the interests of heaven. In such arrangement and harmony is found not only the best line of action for each power, but also the most opportune and efficacious method of helping men in all that pertains to their life here, and to their hope of salvation hereafter. . . . When the civil power is on friendly terms with the sacred authority of the Church, there accrues to both a great increase of usefulness. The dignity of the one is exalted, and so long as religion is its guide it will never rule unjustly; while the other receives help of protection and defence for the public good of the faithful [Leo XIII, 1880, *Arcanum; SW*, I, 41–43].

Pius XI states that the Church has been appointed teacher of the truth, that in matters pertaining to wedlock and moral conduct an inspired teacher is needed, and that the faithful should humbly submit to the will of God.

For the preservation of the moral order neither the laws and sanctions of the temporal power are sufficient, nor is the beauty of virtue and the expounding of its necessity. Religious authority must enter in to enlighten the mind, to direct the will, and to strengthen human frailty by the assistance of divine grace. Such an authority is found nowhere save in the Church instituted by Christ the Lord.

*   *   *

. . . We have admired with due reverence what the all-wise Creator and Redeemer of the human race has ordained with regard to human marriage. At the same time we have expressed Our grief that such a pious ordinance of the divine goodness should today, and on every side, be frustrated and trampled upon by the passions, errors, and vices of men.

*   *   *

. . . It behooves us, above all else, to call to mind that firmly established principle, esteemed alike in sound philosophy and sacred theology: namely, that whatever things have deviated from their right order, cannot be brought back to that original state which is in harmony with their nature except by a return to the divine plan which, as the Angelic Doctor teaches, is the exemplar of all right order.

*   *   *

And how wisely this has been decreed, St. Augustine thus shows: "This indeed is fitting, that the lower be subject to the higher, so that he who would have subject to himself whatever is below him, should himself submit to whatever is above him. Acknowledge order, seek peace. Be thou subject to God, and thy flesh subject to thee. . . . If, however, thou despiseth the subjection of thyself to God, thou shalt never bring about the subjection of the flesh to thyself. If thou dost not obey the Lord, thou shalt be tormented by thy servant" (Ennar. in Ps. 143).

This right ordering on the part of God's wisdom is mentioned by the holy Doctor of the Gentiles, inspired by the Holy Ghost, for in speaking of those ancient philosophers who refused to adore and reverence Him whom they knew to be the Creator of the Universe, he says: "Therefore God has given them up in the lustful desires of their heart to uncleanness, so that they dishonor their own bodies among themselves"; and again: "For this cause God has given them up to shameful lusts" (Rom. 1:24, 26). And St. James says: "God resists the proud but gives grace to the humble" (James 4:6), without which grace, as the same Doctor of the Gentiles reminds us, man cannot subdue the rebellion of his flesh (Rom. 7, 8).

Consequently, as the onslaughts of these uncontrolled passions cannot in any way be lessened, unless the spirit first shows a humble compliance of duty and reverence toward its Maker, it is above all and before all needful that those who are joined in the bond of sacred wedlock should be wholly imbued with a profound and genuine sense of duty toward God, which will shape their whole lives, and fill their minds and wills with a very deep reverence for the majesty of God.

*   *   *

This conformity of wedlock and moral conduct with the divine laws bearing upon marriage, without which its effective restoration cannot be brought about, supposes, however, that all can discern readily, with real certainty, and without any accompanying error, what those laws are. But everyone can see to how many fallacies an avenue would be opened up and how many errors would become mixed with the truth, if it were left solely to the light of reason of each to find it out, or if it were to be discovered by the private interpretation of the truth which is revealed. And if this is applicable to many other truths of the moral order, we must all the more pay attention to those things which appertain to marriage where the inordinate desire for pleasure can attack frail human nature and easily deceive it and lead it astray; this is all the more true of the observance of the divine law, which demands sometimes hard and repeated sacrifices, for which, as experience points out, a weak man can find so many excuses for avoiding the fulfillment of the divine law.

On this account, in order that no falsification or corruption of the divine law but a true, genuine knowledge of it may enlighten the minds of men and guide their conduct, it is necessary that a filial and humble obedience toward the Church should be combined with devotedness to God and the desire of submitting to Him. For Christ Himself made the Church the teacher of truth in those things also which concern the right regulation of moral conduct, even though some knowledge of the same is not beyond human reason. For just as God, in the case of the natural truths of religion and morals, added revelation to the light of reason so that what is right and true, "in the present state also of the human race may be known readily with real certainty without any admixture of error" (Conc. Vat., Sess. iii, 2), so for the same purpose He has constituted the Church the guardian and the teacher of the whole of the truth concerning religion and moral conduct. To her therefore should the faithful show obedience and subject their minds and hearts so as to be kept unharmed and free from error and moral corruption, and so that they shall not deprive themselves of that assistance given by God with such liberal bounty, they ought to show this due obedience not only when the Church defines something with solemn judgment, but also, in proper proportion, when by the constitutions and decrees of the Holy See, opinions are proscribed and condemned as dangerous or distorted (*ibid.,* 4; *Cod. Jur. Can.,* c. 1324).

*   *   *

. . . A characteristic of all true followers of Christ, lettered and unlettered, is to suffer themselves to be guided and led in all things that touch upon faith or morals by the holy Church of God through its Supreme Pastor the Roman Pontiff, who is himself guided by Jesus Christ our Lord [Pius XI, 1930, CC; *SW,* II, 171, 159–163].

Like Leo XIII, Pius XI also asks the state to co-operate with the Church in safeguarding Christian marriage. He says:

There will be no peril to or lessening of the rights and integrity of the state from its association with the Church. Such suspicion and fear is empty and groundless. . . .

*   *   *

Governments can assist the Church greatly in the execution of its important office, if, in laying down their ordinances, they take account of what is prescribed by divine and ecclesiastical law, and if penalties are fixed for offenders. For as it is, there are those who think that whatever is permitted by the laws of the state, or at least is not punished by them, is allowed also in the moral order, and, because they neither fear God nor see any reason to fear the laws of man, they act even against their conscience, thus often bringing ruin upon themselves and upon many others.

*   *   *

. . . Hence We earnestly exhort in the Lord all those who hold the reins of power that they establish and maintain firmly harmony and friendship with this Church of Christ so that, through the united activity and energy of both powers, the tremendous evils, fruits of those wanton liberties which assail both marriage and the family and are a menace to both Church and state, may be effectively frustrated.

*   *   *

To bring forward a recent and clear example of what is meant, it has happened quite in consonance with right order and entirely according to the law of Christ, that in the solemn convention happily entered into between the Holy See and the Kingdom of Italy, a peaceful settlement and friendly co-operation has been obtained even in matrimonial matters, such as befitted the glorious history of the Italian people and its ancient and sacred traditions. These decrees are to be found in the Lateran Pact: "The Italian State, desirous of restoring to the institution of matrimony, which is the basis of the family, that dignity conformable to the traditions of its people, assigns as civil effects of the sacrament of matrimony all that is attributed to it in canon law." To this fundamental norm are added further clauses in the common pact.

This might well be a striking example to all of how, even in this our own day (in which, sad to say, the absolute separation of the civil power from the Church, and indeed from every religion, is so often taught), one supreme authority can be united and associated with the other without detriment to the rights and supreme power of either, thus protecting Christian parents from pernicious evils and menacing ruin [Pius XI, 1930, CC: *SW*, II, 171–172].

MIXED MARRIAGE

Leo XIII denounces and cites the dangers of mixed marriages.
Care must also be taken that they do not easily enter into marriage with those who are not Catholics; for when minds do

not agree as to the observances of religion, it is scarcely possible to hope for agreement in other things. Other reasons which also prove that persons should turn with dread from such marriages are chiefly these: that such marriages give occasion to forbidden association and communion in religious matters; that they endanger the faith of the Catholic partners; that they are a hindrance to the proper education of the children; and that they often lead to a confused concept of truth and falsehood, and to the belief that all religions are equally good [Leo XIII, 1880, *Arcanum; SW*, I, 45].

Pius XI states the Church's law concerning mixed marriage; he indicates the evil effects of such a marriage and maintains that it lacks a close union of spirit.

They, therefore, who rashly and heedlessly contract mixed marriages, from which the maternal love and providence of the Church dissuades her children for very sound reasons, fail conspicuously in this respect, sometimes with danger to their eternal salvation. This attitude of the Church to mixed marriage appears in many of her documents, all of which are summed up in the Code of Canon Law: "Everywhere and with the greatest strictness the Church forbids marriage between baptized persons, one of whom is a Catholic and the other a member of a schismatical or heretical sect; and if there is added to this the danger of the falling away of the Catholic party and the perversion of the children, such a marriage is forbidden also by the divine law" (*Cod. Jur. Can.*, c. 1060). If the Church occasionally on account of circumstances does not refuse to grant a dispensation from these strict laws (provided that the divine law remains intact and the dangers above mentioned are provided against by suitable safeguards), it is unlikely that the Catholic party will not suffer some detriment from such a marriage.

Whence it comes about not infrequently, as experience shows, that deplorable defections from religion occur among the offspring, or at least a headlong descent into that religious indifference which is closely allied to impiety. There is this also to be considered that in these mixed marriages it becomes much more difficult to imitate by a lively conformity of spirit the mystery of which We have spoken, namely, that close union between Christ and His Church.

Assuredly, also, will there be wanting that close union of spirit which as it is the sign and mark of the Church of Christ, so also should be the sign of Christian wedlock, its glory and adornment. For, where there exists diversity of mind, truth, and feeling, the bond of union of mind and heart is wont to be broken, or at least weakened. From this comes the danger lest the love of man and wife grow cold and the peace and happiness of family life, resting as it does on the union of hearts, be destroyed. Many centuries ago indeed, the old Roman law had proclaimed: "Marriages are the union of male and female, a sharing of life and the communication of divine and human rights" [Pius XI, 1930, CC; *SW*, II, 154].

A thorough training in the Catholic religion is a powerful safeguard to mixed marriage, states Pope Pius XII.

With regard to those marriages in which one or the other party does not accept the Catholic teaching or has not been baptized, We are certain that you observe exactly the prescriptions of the Code of Canon Law. Such marriages, in fact, as is clear to you from wide experience, are rarely happy and usually occasion grave loss to the Catholic Church.

A very efficacious means for driving out such grave evils is that individual Catholics receive a thorough training in the Divine truths and that the people be shown clearly the road which leads to salvation [Pius XII, 1939, *Sertum Laetitiae; CM,* XXXVII, 933].

CATHOLICS AND CIVIL MARRIAGE

Pope Leo XIII states that a marriage of Catholics which is not a sacrament is no real marriage; but, at the same time, he wants Catholics to conform to state laws which are in harmony with the laws of the Church.

. . . All ought to understand clearly that, if there be any union of a man and woman among the faithful of Christ which is not a sacrament, such union has not the force and nature of a proper marriage; that although contracted in accordance with the laws of the State, it cannot be more than a rite or custom introduced by the civil law. Further, the civil law can deal with and decide those matters alone which in the civil order spring from marriage, and which cannot possibly exist, as is evident, unless there be a true and lawful cause for them, that is to say, the nuptial bond. It is of the greatest consequence to the husband and wife that all these things should be known and well understood by them, in order that they may conform to the laws of the State, if there be no objection on the part of the Church; for the Church wishes the effects of marriage to be guarded in all possible ways, and that no harm may come to the children [Leo XIII, 1880, *Arcanum; SW*, I, 44]. **1104148**

Concerning civil authority and marriage, Pius XII writes:

. . . There can be no doubt, as everyone knows, that the civil authority has jurisdiction in matters regarding the purely civil effects of marriage (Canon 1016) . . . [Pius XII, 1946, *On Faith and Marriage; CM*, XLV, 133].

In a radio message to Austrian Catholics in Vienna, Pius XII said:

. . . You must uphold the sanctity of marriage. Let the nuptial ceremony be always sacred to you. A Catholic can enter a true marriage only with the blessing of the Church and not through a purely civil ceremony . . . [Pius XII, 1952, *To Austrian Catholics; CM*, LI, 49].

SECULARIZATION OF MARRIAGE

Leo XIII sees in secularization of marriage the great evil it really is, and he denounces it most vehemently.

. . . When impious laws, without regard to the respect due this great sacrament, place it in the same category as purely civil contracts, deplorable consequences follow. Thus the dignity of Christian marriage has been violated, citizens have substituted legal concubinage for the legitimate union, married couples have neglected their mutual duties of fidelity, children have not observed the respect and obedience due their parents, the ties of domestic affection have been relaxed, and — as a most detestable example and gravest prejudice to public morals — pernicious and regrettable separations have very often succeeded an insensate love . . . [Leo XIII, 1878, *Inscrutabili; SW*, I, 10].

They debase the natural union of man and woman, which is held sacred even among barbarous peoples; and its bond, by which the family is chiefly held together, they weaken, or even deliver up to lust [Leo XIII, 1878, *Quod Apostolici Muneris; SW*, I, 15].

Yet owing to the efforts of the archenemy of mankind, there are persons who, thanklessly casting away so many other blessings of redemption, despise also or utterly ignore the restoration of marriage to its original perfection. It is the reproach of some of the ancients that they showed themselves the enemies of marriage in many ways; but, in our own age, much more pernicious is the sin of those who would fain pervert utterly the nature of marriage, perfect though it is, and complete in all its details and parts. The chief reason why they act in this way is because very many, imbued with the maxims of a false philosophy and corrupted in morals, judge nothing so unbearable as submission and obedience. They strive with all their might to bring about that not only individual men, but families also, nay indeed human society itself, may in haughty pride despise the sovereignty of God.

Now, since the family and human society at large spring from marriage, these men will on no account allow matrimony to be subject to the jurisdiction of the Church. Nay, they endeavour to deprive it of all holiness, and so bring it within the contracted sphere of those rights which, having been instituted by man, are ruled and administered by the civil jurisprudence of the community. Wherefore it necessarily follows that they attribute all power over marriage to civil rulers, and allow none whatever to the Church. When the Church exercises any such power, they think that she acts either by favour of the civil authority or to its injury. Now is the time, they say, for the heads of the State to vindicate their rights unflinchingly, and to do their best to settle all that relates to marriage according as to them seems good.

Hence are owing civil marriages, commonly so called; hence laws are framed which impose impediments to marriage; hence arise judicial sentences affecting the marriage contract, as to whether or not it has been rightly made. Lastly, all power of prescribing and passing judgement in this kind of cause is, as we see, of set purpose denied to the Catholic Church, so that no regard is paid either to her divine power or to her prudent laws. Yet under these, for so many centuries, have the nations lived on whom the light of civilization shone bright with the wisdom of Christ Jesus.

*   *   *

. . . But now there is spreading a wish to supplant natural and divine law by human law; and hence has begun a gradual extinction of that most excellent ideal of marriage which nature herself had impressed on the soul of man, and sealed, as it were, with her own seal. Nay, more, even in Christian marriages this power, productive of such great good, has been weakened by the sinfulness of man. Of what advantage is it if a State can institute nuptials estranged from the Christian religion, when she is the true mother of all good, cherishing all sublime virtues, quickening and urging us to everything that constitutes the glory of a lofty and generous soul? With the rejection and repudiation of the Christian religion, marriage sinks of necessity into the slavery of man's vicious nature and vile passions, and finds but little protection in the help of natural goodness. A very torrent of evil has flowed from this source, not only into private families, but also into states. For when the salutary fear of God is removed, and there remains no longer that refreshment in toil which is nowhere more abounding than in the Christian religion, it very often happens, as indeed is evident, that the mutual services and duties of marriages seem almost unbearable. Thus it comes about that very many yearn to loosen the tie which they regard as woven by human law and made out of their own will, whenever incompatibility of temper, or quarrels, or the violation of the marriage vow, or mutual consent, or other reasons induce them to think that it would be well to be set free. Then, if they are hindered by law from carrying out this shameless desire, they contend that the laws are iniquitous, inhuman, and at variance with the rights of free citizens; adding that every effort should be made to repeal such enactments, and to introduce a more humane code sanctioning divorce.

*   *   *

. . . The fact is that in the projects and enactments of men there exists no power that can change the character and tendency given to things by nature. Those men, therefore, show but little wisdom in the idea they have formed of the well-being of the commonwealth, who think that the inherent character of marriage can be perverted with impunity; and who, disregarding the sanctity of religion and of the sacrament, seemingly wish to degrade and dishonour marriage more basely than was done even under heathen laws. Indeed, without some change in these views, both private families and public society in its entirety may well restlessly fear lest they should be miserably driven into that general welter and overthrow of order which even now it is the evil aim of Socialists and Communists to bring about [Leo XIII, 1880, *Arcanum; SW,* I, 32–33, 37–38, 40].

Pius XI deplores the modern attack and the destructive propaganda on the Christian ideal of marriage. He writes:

When we consider the great excellence of chaste wedlock, Venerable Brethren, it appears all the more regrettable that particularly in our day we should witness this divine institution often scorned and on every side degraded.

For today, alas, not secretly nor under cover, but openly, with all sense of shame put aside, now by word, again by writings, by theatrical productions of every kind, by romantic fiction, by amorous and frivolous novels, by cinematographs portraying in vivid scene, in addresses broadcast by means of the radio, in short by all the inventions of modern science, the sanctity of marriage is trampled upon and derided; divorce, adultery, all the basest vices either are extolled or at least are depicted in such colors as to appear to be free of all reproach and infamy. Books are not lacking which dare to proclaim themselves scientific but which in truth are merely coated with a veneer of science in order that they may the more easily insinuate their ideas. The doctrines defended in these are offered for sale as the productions of modern genius, of that genius namely, which, anxious only for truth, is considered to have emancipated itself from all those old-fashioned and immature opinions of the ancients. And to the number of these antiquated opinions they relegate the traditional doctrine of Christian marriage.

These thoughts are instilled into men of every class, rich and poor, masters and workers, lettered and unlettered, married and single, the godly and godless, old and young, but for these last, as easiest prey, the worst snares are laid.

Not all the sponsors of these new doctrines are swept away to the extremes of unbridled lust. There are those who, striving as it were to ride a middle course, believe nevertheless that something should be conceded in our times as regards certain precepts of the divine and natural law. But these likewise, more or less wittingly, are emissaries of the great enemy who is ever seeking to sow weeds among the wheat (Mt. 13:25). . . .

*   *   *

To begin at the very source of these evils, their basic principle lies in this, that matrimony is repeatedly declared to be not instituted by the Author of nature nor raised by Christ the Lord to the dignity of a true sacrament, but invented by man. Some confidently assert that they have found no evidence for the existence of matrimony in nature or in her laws, but regard it merely as the means of producing life and of gratifying in one way or another a vehement impulse; on the other hand, others recognize that certain beginnings or, as it were, seeds of true wedlock are found in the nature of man since, unless men were bound together by some form of permanent tie, the dignity of husband and wife or the natural end of propagating and rearing the offspring would not receive satisfactory provision. At the same time they maintain that in all beyond this germinal idea matrimony, through various concurrent causes, is invented solely by the mind of man, established solely by his will.

How grievously all these err and how shamelessly they leave the ways of honesty is already evident from what we have set forth here regarding the origin and nature of wedlock, its purposes, and the good inherent in it. The evil of this teaching is plainly seen from the consequences which its advocates deduce from it, namely, that the laws, institutions, and customs by which wedlock is governed, since they take their origin solely from the will of man, are subject entirely to him, hence can and must be founded, changed, and abrogated according to human caprice and the shifting circumstances of human affairs; that the generative power which is grounded in nature itself is more sacred and has wider range than matrimony — hence it may be exercised both outside as well as within the confines of wedlock, even though the purpose of matrimony be set aside, as though to suggest that the license of a base fornicating woman should enjoy the same rights as the chaste motherhood of a lawfully wedded wife.

*   *   *

. . . They put forward in the first place that matrimony belongs entirely to the profane and purely civil sphere, that it is not to be committed to the religious society, the Church of Christ, but to civil society alone. They then add that the marriage contract is to be freed from any indissoluble bond, and that separation and divorce are not only to be tolerated but sanctioned by the law; from which it follows finally that, robbed of all its holiness, matrimony should be enumerated among the secular and civil institutions.

The first point is contained in their contention that the civil act itself should stand for the marriage contract (civil matrimony, as it is called), while the religious act is to be considered a mere addition, or at most a concession to a too superstitious people. Moreover they want it to be no cause for reproach that marriages be contracted by Catholics with non-Catholics without any reference to religion or recourse to the ecclesiastical authorities. The second point, which is but a consequence of the first is to be found in their excuse for complete divorce and in their praise and encouragement of those civil laws which favor the loosening of the bond itself [Pius XI, 1930, CC; *SW*, II, 140–142, 152].

Pius XI, referring to the modern state, writes:
. . . Neither God nor Christ our Lord are any longer considered as presiding over the family. Matrimony, now a mere civil contract, is no longer regarded as that "great mystery" (Eph. 5:32) which Christ instituted and which He wished to be the holy and sanctifying symbol of that indissoluble bond which unites Him with His Church. On all sides we see the idea of religion obscured among the people, and that religious sense blunted which the Church has implanted in the family, as the nucleus of society. Domestic order and domestic peace are overthrown, the unity and stability of the family injured, and its sanctity violated by the lust of sordid passion and the fatal attachment to empty gain, with the result that the very springs of life, both of the family and of the race, are polluted [Pius XI, 1922, *Ubi Arcano; SW*, II, 13].

Pope Pius XII states that the rejection of Christ means darkness and disorder, and the consequences are:
. . . that the moral values by which in other times public and private conduct was gauged have fallen into disuse; and the much vaunted civilization of society, which has made ever more rapid progress, withdrawing man, the family and the State from the beneficent and regenerating effects of the idea of God and the teaching of the Church, has caused to reappear, in regions in which for many centuries shone the splendors of Christian civilization, in a manner ever clearer, ever more distinct, ever more distressing, the signs of a corrupt and corrupting paganism . . . [Pius XII, 1939, *Summi Pontificatus; CM*, XXXVII, 897].

The vices of our day due to irreligion are the following, writes Pius XII:

. . . levity in entering into marriage, divorce, the break-up of the family, the cooling of mutual affection between parents and children, birth control, the enfeeblement of the race, the weakening of respect for authority . . . [Pius XII, 1939, *Sertum Laetitiae; CM,* XXXVII, 931].

EMANCIPATION OF WOMAN

Pius XI denounces the false "emancipation" of the wife from the husband, the home, and the children.

The same false teachers who try to dim the luster of conjugal faith and purity do not scruple to do away with the honorable and trusting obedience which the woman owes to the man. Many of them even go further and assert that such a subjection of one party to the other is unworthy of human dignity, that the rights of husband and wife are equal; wherefore, they boldly proclaim, the emancipation of women has been or ought to be effected. This emancipation in their ideas must be threefold, in the ruling of the domestic society, in the administration of family affairs, and in the rearing of the children. It must be social, economic, physiological, that is to say, the woman is to be freed at her own good pleasure from the burdensome duties properly belonging to a wife as companion and mother (We have already said that this is not an emancipation but a crime); social, inasmuch as the wife being freed from the care of children and family, should, to the neglect of these, be able to follow her own bent and devote herself to business and even public affairs; finally economic, whereby the woman even without the knowledge and against the wish of her husband may be at liberty to conduct and administer her own affairs, giving her attention chiefly to these rather than to children, husband, and family.

This, however, is not the true emancipation of woman, nor that rational and exalted liberty which belongs to the noble office of a Christian woman and wife; it is rather the debasing of the womanly character and the dignity of motherhood, and indeed of the whole family, as a result of which the husband suffers the loss of his wife, the children of their mother, and the home and the whole family of an ever watchful guardian. More than this, this false liberty and unnatural equality with the husband is to the detriment of the woman herself, for if the woman descends from her truly regal throne to which she has been raised with the walls of the home by means of the Gospel, she will soon be reduced to the old state of slavery (if not in appearance, certainly in reality) and become as among the pagans the mere instrument of man [Pius XI, 1930, CC; *SW*, II, 150–151].

Speaking about the modern emancipation of woman and her equality of rights with man, Pius XII asks: "Has woman's position been thereby improved?" Then he writes:

Equality of rights with man brought with it her abandonment of the home where she reigned as queen, and her subjection to the same work strain and working hours. It entails depreciation of her true dignity and the solid foundation of all her rights which is her characteristic feminine role, and the intimate coordination of the two sexes. The end intended by God for the good of all human society, especially for the family, is lost sight of. In concessions made to woman one can easily see not respect for her dignity or her mission, but an attempt to foster the economic and military power of the totalitarian state to which all must inexorably be subordinated.

On the other hand, can a woman, perhaps, hope for her real well-being from a regime dominated by capitalism? We do not need to describe to you now the economic and social results that issue from it. You know its characteristic signs, and you yourselves are bearing its burden: excessive concentration of populations in cities, the constant all-absorbing increase of big industries, the difficult and precarious state of others, notably those of artisan and agricultural workers, and the disturbing increase of unemployment.

To restore as far as possible the honor of the woman's and

mother's place in the home: that is the watchword one hears now from many quarters like a cry of alarm, as if the world were awakening, terrified by the fruits of material and scientific progress of which it before was so proud [Pius XII, 1945, *Woman's Duties in Social and Political Life; CM*, XLIII, 709].

COMPANIONATE MARRIAGE

Pius XI, when speaking about modern fallacies and new species of unions, says:

. . . Some men go so far as to concoct new species of unions, suited, as they say, to the present temper of men and the times, which various new forms of matrimony they presume to label "temporary," "experimental," and "companionate." These offer all the indulgence of matrimony and its rights without, however, the indissoluble bond, and without offspring, unless later the parties alter their cohabitation into a matrimony in the full sense of the law.

Indeed there are some who desire and insist that these practices be legitimized by the law or, at least, excused by their general acceptance among the people. They do not seem even to suspect that these proposals partake of nothing of the modern "culture" in which they glory so much, but are simply hateful abominations which beyond all question reduce our truly cultured nations to the barbarous standards of savage peoples [Pius XI, 1930, CC; *SW*, II, 142–143].

INCOMPATIBILITY

Incompatibility is a sin against conjugal faith, concerning which Pius XI writes:

These enemies of marriage go further, however, when they substitute for that true and solid love, which is the basis of conjugal happiness, a certain vague compatibility of temperament. This they call sympathy and assert that, since it is the only bond by which husband and wife are linked together, when it ceases the marriage is completely dissolved. What else is this than to build a house upon sand? — a house that in the words of Christ would forthwith be shaken and collapse, as soon as it was exposed to the waves of adversity "and the winds blew and beat against that house, and it fell, and was utterly ruined" (Mt. 7:27). On the other hand, the house built upon a rock, that is to say on mutual conjugal chastity, and strengthened by the deliberate and constant union of spirit, will not only never fall away but will never be shaken by adversity [Pius XI, 1930, CC; SW, II, 152].

DIVORCE

Concerning divorce, one of the great evils of society, due to the secularization of marriage, Leo XIII writes:

. . . When impious laws, without regard to the respect due this great sacrament, place it in the same category as purely civil contracts, deplorable consequences follow. Thus the dignity of Christian marriage has been violated, citizens have substituted legal concubinage for the legitimate union, married couples have neglected their mutual duties of fidelity, children have not observed the respect and obedience due their parents, the ties of domestic affection have been relaxed, and — as a most detestable example and gravest prejudice to public morals — pernicious and regrettable separations have very often succeeded an insensate love [Leo XIII, 1878, *Inscrutabili; SW*, I, 10].

Now, however much the legislators of these our days may wish to guard themselves against the impiety of men such as here referred to, they are unable to do so, since they profess to hold and defend the very same principles of jurisprudence. Hence they comply with the times, and render divorce easily obtainable. History itself illustrates this. To pass over other instances, we find that at the close of the last century divorces were sanctioned by law in that upheaval, or as we might better call it, conflagration in France, when society was wholly degraded by its abandoning of God. Many at the present time would fain have those laws re-enacted, because they wish God and His Church to be altogether exiled and excluded from the midst of human society, madly imagining that in such laws a final remedy must be sought for the moral corruption which is advancing with rapid strides.

Truly, it is hardly possible to describe the magnitude of the evils that flow from divorce. Matrimonial contracts are by it made variable, mutual kindness is weakened, deplorable inducements to unfaithfulness are supplied, harm is done to the education and training of children, occasion is afforded for the breaking up of homes, the seeds of dissension are sown among families, the dignity of womanhood is lessened and brought low, and women run the risk of being deserted after having ministered to the pleasures of men. Since, then, nothing has such power to lay waste families and destroy the mainstay of kingdoms as the corruption of morals, it is easily seen that divorces are in the highest degree hostile to the prosperity of families and states, springing as they do from the depraved morals of the people, and, as experience shows us, opening out a way to every kind of evil-doing in public as well as in private life.

Further still, if the matter be duly pondered, we shall clearly see that these evils are the more especially dangerous, because when divorce has once been tolerated, no restraint is powerful enough to keep it within the bounds marked out or presurmised. Great indeed is the force of example, and even greater still the might of passion. With such incitements it must needs follow that the eagerness for divorce which daily spreads in devious ways, will infect the minds of many like a virulent contagious disease, or like a flood of water will burst through every barrier.

These truths, doubtless, are clear enough in themselves. But they will become still clearer if we call to mind the teachings of experience. No sooner has the road to divorce begun to be made smooth by law, than at once quarrels, jealousies, and judicial separations largely increase. Upon this so great a shamelessness of life follows as to make even those who previously had favoured the divorces repent of their action lest, if a remedy is not sedulously sought, by repealing the law, the State itself might come to ruin.

The Romans of old are said to have shrunk with horror from the first examples of divorce, but ere long, all sense of decency was blunted in their soul. The meagre restraint of passion died out, and the marriage vow was so often broken that the statement of some writers would actually seem to have been true — namely, that women used to reckon years not by the change of Consuls, but of their husbands.

In like manner Protestants at first allowed legalized divorces in certain but as yet few cases. With the occurrence, however, of circumstances of a similar kind, the number of divorces spread to such an extent in Germany, America, and elsewhere, that all wise thinkers deplored the limitlessness of the laws as simply intolerable. Even in Catholic states the like evil existed. Whereever at any time divorce was introduced, the abundance of misery that followed far exceeded anything the framers of the law could have foreseen. In fact, many applied their minds to contriving all kinds of frauds and devices, bringing accusations of cruelty, violence, and adultery merely to feign grounds for the dissolution of the matrimonial bond of which they had grown weary. As a result of all this so great a havoc in morals followed that an amendment of the laws was regarded as urgently needed.

*　　*　　*

Thus, we clearly see how foolish and senseless it is to expect any public good from divorce. On the contrary, its obvious tendency is the certain destruction of society [Leo XIII, 1880, *Arcanum; SW*, I, 38–41].

Leo XIII points out that Christ condemned the Jewish custom of giving bills of divorce, granting the right of remarriage, and he also states that partial divorce is permitted by the Catholic Church.

. . . He [Christ] brought back matrimony to the nobility of its primevil origin by condemning the customs of the Jews in their abuse of the plurality of wives and of the power of giving bills of divorce; and still more by commanding most strictly that no one should dare to dissolve that union which God Himself had sanctioned by a bond perpetual. Hence, after setting aside the difficulties which were adduced from the law of Moses, he thus decreed, in the character of Supreme Lawgiver, concerning husbands and wives: "I say to you, that whosoever shall put away his wife, except it be for fornication, and shall marry another, committeth adultery; and he that shall marry her that is put away committeth adultery" (Mt. 19:9).

*　　*　　*

. . . Those husbands and wives are guilty of a manifest crime who plan, for whatsoever reason, to be united in a second marriage before the first one has been ended by death. When, indeed, matters have come to such a pitch that it seems impossible for them to live together any longer, then the Church allows them to live apart, and strives at the same time to soften the evils of this separation by such remedies and helps as are suited to their condition; yet she never ceases to endeavour to bring about a reconciliation, and never despairs of doing so. But these are extreme cases; and they would seldom exist if men and women entered into the married state with proper dispositions, not influenced by passion, but entertaining right ideas of the duties of marriage and of its noble purpose; neither would they anticipate their marriage by a series of sins drawing down upon them the wrath of God [Leo XIII, 1880, *Arcanum; SW*, I, 28–29, 44].

Pope Pius XI absolutely disavows divorce, brands it a menace to society, and points out that "the daily increasing facility of divorce is an obstacle to the restoration of marriage to that state of perfection which the Divine Redeemer willed it should possess" (*1930, CC;* SW, *II, 155*).

The advocates of the neopaganism of today have learned nothing from the sad state of affairs, but instead, day by day, more and more vehemently, they continue by legislation to attack the indissolubility of the marriage bond, proclaiming that the lawfulness of divorce must be recognized, and that the antiquated laws should give place to a new and more humane legislation.

Many and varied are the grounds put forward for divorce,

some arising from the wickedness and the guilt of the persons concerned, others arising from the circumstances of the case; the former they describe as subjective, the latter as objective; in a word, whatever might make married life hard or unpleasant. They strive to prove their contentions regarding these grounds for the divorce legislation they would bring about, by various arguments. Thus, in the first place, they maintain that it is for the good of either party that the one who is innocent should have the right to separate from the guilty, or that the guilty should be withdrawn from a union which is unpleasing to him and against his will. In the second place, they argue, the good of the child demands this, for either it will be deprived of a proper education or the natural fruits of it, and will too easily be affected by the discords and shortcomings of the parents, and drawn from the path of virtue. And thirdly the common good of society requires that these marriages should be completely dissolved, which are now incapable of producing their natural results, and that legal separations should be allowed when crimes are to be feared as the result of the common habitation and intercourse of the parties. This last, they say, must be admitted to avoid the crimes being committed purposely with a view to obtaining the desired sentence of divorce for which the judge can legally loose the marriage bond, as also to prevent people from coming before the courts when it is obvious from the state of the case that they are lying and perjuring themselves — all of which brings the court and the lawful authority into contempt. Hence the civil laws, in their opinion, have to be reformed to meet these new requirements, to suit the changes of the times and the changes in men's opinions, civil institutions, and customs. Each of these reasons is considered by them as conclusive, so that all taken together offer a clear proof of the necessity of granting divorce in certain cases.

Others, taking a step further, simply state that marriage, being a private contract, is, like other private contracts, to be left to the consent and good pleasure of both parties, and so can be dissolved for any reason whatsoever.

Opposed to all these reckless opinions, Venerable Brethren, stands the unalterable law of God, fully confirmed by Christ, a law that can never be deprived of its force by the decrees of men, the ideas of a people, or the will of any legislator: "What therefore God has joined together, let no man put asunder" (Mt. 19:6). And if any man, acting contrary to this law, shall have put asunder, his action is null and void, and the consequence remains, as Christ Himself has explicitly confirmed: "Everyone who puts away his wife and marries another, commits adultery: and he who marries a woman who has been put away from her husband commits adultery" (Lk. 16:18). Moreover, these words refer to every kind of marriage, even that which is natural and legitimate only; for, as has already been observed, that indissolubility by which the loosening of the bond is once and for all removed from the whim of the parties and from every secular power, is a property of every true marriage.

Let that solemn pronouncement of the Council of Trent be recalled to mind in which, under the stigma of anathema, it condemned these errors: "If anyone should say that on account of heresy or the hardships of cohabitation or a deliberate abuse of one party by the other the marriage tie may be loosened, let him be anathema" (Conc. Trid., Sess. xxiv, 5) and again: "If anyone should say that the Church errs in having taught or in teaching that, according to the doctrine of the Gospel and the Apostles, the bond of marriage cannot be loosed because of the sin of adultery of either party; or that neither party, even though he be innocent, having given no cause for the sin of adultery, can contract another marriage during the life time of the other; and that he commits adultery who marries another after putting away his adulterous wife, and likewise that she commits adultery who puts away her husband and marries another: let him be anathema" (*ibid.* 7).

If therefore the Church has not erred and does not err in teaching this, and if consequently it is certain that the bond of marriage cannot be loosed even on account of the sin of adultery, it is evident that all the other weaker excuses that can be, and are usually brought forward are of no value whatsoever.

And the objections brought against the firmness of the marriage bond, on the grounds mentioned, are easily answered. For, in certain circumstances, imperfect separation of the parties is allowed, the bond not being severed. This separation, which the Church herself permits, and expressly mentions in her canon law in those canons which deal with the separation of the parties as to marital relationship and cohabitation, removes all the alleged inconveniences and dangers (*Cod. Jur. Can.*, cc. 1128 sqq.). It will be for the sacred law and, to some extent, also the civil law, in so far as civil matters are affected, to lay down the grounds, the conditions, the method and precautions to be taken in a case of this kind in order to safeguard the education of the children and the well-being of the family, and to remove all those evils which threaten the married persons, the children, and the state.

Now all those arguments that are brought forward to prove the indissolubility of the marriage tie, arguments which have already been touched upon, can equally be applied to excluding not only the necessity of divorce, but even the power to grant it; while for all the advantages that can be put forward for the former, there can be adduced as many disadvantages and evils which are a formidable menace to the whole of human society.

To revert again to the expressions of Our predecessor, it is hardly necessary to point out what an amount of good is involved in the absolute indissolubility of wedlock and what a train of evils follows upon divorce. Whenever the marriage bond remains intact, then we find marriages contracted with a sense of safety and security, while, when separations are considered and the dangers of divorce are present, the marriage contract itself becomes insecure, or at least gives ground for anxiety and surprises. On the one hand we see a wonderful strengthening of good will and co-operation in the daily life of husband and wife, while, on the other, both of these are miserably weakened by the presence of a facility for divorce. Here we have at a very opportune moment a source of help by which both parties are enabled to preserve their purity and loyalty; there we find harmful inducements to unfaithfulness. On this side we find the birth of children and their tuition and upbringing effectively promoted, many avenues of discord closed among families and relations, and the beginnings of rivalry and jealousy easily suppressed; on that, very great obstacles to the birth and rearing of children and their education, and many occasions of quarrels, and seeds of jealousy sown everywhere. Finally, but especially, the dignity and position of women in civil and domestic society is reinstated by the former; while by the latter it is shamefully lowered and the danger is incurred of their being considered outcasts, slaves of the lust of men (*Arcanum*).

To conclude with the important words of Leo XIII, since the destruction of family life "and the loss of national wealth is brought about more by the corruption of morals than by anything else, it is easily seen that divorce, which is born of the perverted morals of a people, and leads, as experiment shows, to vicious habits in public and private life, is particularly opposed to the well-being of the family and of the state. The serious nature of these evils will be the more clearly recognized, when we remember that, once divorce has been allowed, there will be no sufficient means of keeping it in check within any definite bounds. Great is the force of example, greater still that of lust; and with such incitements it cannot but happen that divorce and its consequent setting loose of the passions should spread daily and attack the souls of many like a contagious disease or a river bursting its banks and flooding the land" (*ibid.*).

Thus, as we read in the same letter, "unless things change, the human family and state have every reason to fear lest they should suffer absolute ruin." All this was written fifty years ago, yet it is confirmed by the daily increasing corruption of morals and the unheard-of degradation of the family in those lands where communism reigns unchecked [Pius XI, 1930, CC; *SW*, II, 155–159].

Concerning the Church's determined stand against civil divorce, Pius XII writes to the American hierarchy as follows:

That this capital point of Catholic doctrine is of great value for the solidity of the family structure, for the progress and prosperity of civil society, for the healthy life of the people and for civilization, that its light may not be false, is a fact recognized even by no small number of men who, though estranged from the Faith, are entitled to respect for their political acumen. Oh! If only your country had come to know from the experience of others rather than from examples at home of the accumulation of ills which derive from the plague of divorce; let reverence for religion, let fidelity towards the great American people counsel energetic action that this disease, alas so widespread, may be cured by extirpation.

The consequences of this evil have been thus described by Pope Leo XIII, in words whose truth is incisive: "Because of divorce, the nuptial contract becomes subject to fickle whim; affection is weakened; pernicious incentives are given to conjugal infidelity; the care and education of offspring are harmed; easy opportunity is afforded for the breaking up of homes; the seeds of discord are sown among families; the dignity of woman is lessened and brought down and she runs the risk of being deserted after she has served her husband as an instrument of pleasure. And since it is true that for the ruination of the family and the undermining of the State nothing is so powerful as the corruption of morals, it is easy to see that divorce is of the greatest harm to the prosperity of families and of states" (Encyclical Letter Arcanum) [Pius XII, 1939, *Sertum Laetitiae; CM,* XXXVII, 932].

To the members of the Roman Rota, Pius XII said:

. . . It is true that nowadays, when contempt and neglect of religion have caused the revival of a new pagan spirit, pleasure-loving and impatient of restraint, we find in certain parts of the world a mania for divorce such that people tend to make and unmake marriages with an ease and a lightheartedness which they would eschew in an ordinary contract of hire. But this mania thoughtless and irrational, cannot be regarded by ecclesiastical tribunals as a reason for departing from the norms and practice which are stated and approved by a sound judgment and a God-fearing conscience. For the indissolubility or dissolubility of marriage the only norm and practice which can hold for the Church is that which God, the Author of nature and grace, has established [Pius XII, 1941, "Marriage Legislation"; *Clergy Review, XXII, 87*].

Speaking on the Sacraments to the Pastors of Rome and to the Preachers for the Sacred Time of Lent, Pius XII stated:

As for the Sacrament of Marriage, Italy at present in its legislation does not recognize divorce. And note well that the Church is not the only one who rejects it: even from the world of lay jurists and sociologists there have arisen authoritative voices warning, begging that divorce be not allowed to enter to violate and break up the sanctuary of marriage and of the family.

Alas, however, an open propaganda in favor of divorce has already been begun in a certain section of the press, with danger that the incautious may be led into error and a movement contrary to the natural and divine law, to the holy law of Christ, may be encouraged. Faithful Catholics must therefore keep unshaken the following three fundamental points:

They cannot contract a true valid marriage except according to the form prescribed by the Church.

Marriage validly contracted between baptized persons is by that very fact a Sacrament.

This valid marriage between baptized persons, once consummated, cannot for any cause be dissolved by any human authority, by any power on earth, but only by death.

It is your duty, pastors of souls, to impress profoundly these three principles on the mind and on the conscience of the faithful, so that they may serve them as a rule in their own lives and dictate for them on every occasion a firm and precise line of conduct [Pius XII, 1945, "The Sacraments"; *The Unwearied Advocate*, II, 9–10].

Speaking of civil divorce, Pius XII has this to say to the members of the Ecclesiastical Court of the Rota:

. . . Even where the parties are not baptized, marriage legitimately contracted is a sacred thing in the natural order. The civil courts have no power to dissolve it, and the Church has never recognized the validity of divorce decrees in such cases. . . . [Pius XII, 1946, *On Faith and Marriage; CM*, XLV, 133].

Chapter II

PURPOSE AND FUNCTION OF MARRIAGE

According to traditional Catholic teaching the right to marry is one of the most fundamental of the natural rights of man. And one of the most natural expressions of love between married people is the conjugal act, which under normal circumstances, will result in the generation of offspring.

Anything that is done by the individual or by the State to defeat the natural consequences of the conjugal act is immoral: to practice contraception, to deliberately cause abortion, or to sterilize an individual.

Natural birth limitation is permitted under certain conditions. And if a woman's health is such that pregnancy would seriously endanger her life, complete sexual abstinence, with the help of God's grace, must be practiced.

Artificial insemination in marriage and outside marriage must be branded as immoral.

Euthanasia is a monstrous theory because it extols fatal practices.

Parenthood is a great blessing. Husband and wife should receive their children with joy and gratitude from the hand of God, and they should regard their children as a talent committed to their charge by God, to be restored to God with interest on the day of reckoning. Consequently, parents must jealously guard their authority to educate and care for their children. And in their endeavor to educate their children, parents should honestly try to understand their children's problems.

Thorough instruction in the precepts of religion and character training is imperative for Catholic children. Information pertaining to sex with emphasis on self-mastery and the virtue of modesty should be given. Adolescents will benefit from instructions on the religious character of marriage, the unity, and the indissolubility of marriage.

Mutual love and companionship of the spouses is of paramount importance in married life. And the best means of overcoming the trials of conjugal life is found in the reception of the Sacraments. Happiness in marriage should be sought after because it is a source of great benefit to the individual and to society at large.

In this chapter, then, in addition to restating traditional precepts, the excerpts that follow also illustrate the application of traditional principles to practices which have developed in certain areas of modern family life.

PREPARATION FOR MARRIAGE

Leo XIII stresses the need of instruction. He writes:

Let special care be taken that the people be well instructed in the precepts of Christian wisdom, so that they may always remember that marriage was not instituted by the will of man, but, from the very beginning, by the authority and command of God; that it does not admit of plurality of wives or husbands; that Christ, the author of the New Covenant, raised it from a rite of nature to be a sacrament, and gave to His Church legislative and judicial power with regard to the bond of union. On this point the very greatest care must be taken to instruct them, lest their minds should be led into error by the unsound conclusions of adversaries who desire that the Church should be deprived of that power [Leo XIII, 1880, *Arcanum; SW*, I, 43–44].

Pius XI states:

This religious character of marriage, its sublime signification of grace and the union between Christ and the Church, evidently requires that those about to marry should show a holy reverence toward it, and zealously endeavor to make their marriage approach as nearly as possible to the archetype of Christ and the Church.

*   *   *

. . . It is indeed of the utmost importance that the faithful should be well instructed concerning matrimony; and this both by word of mouth and by the written word, not cursorily but often and fully, by means of plain and weighty arguments, so that these truths will strike the intellect and will be deeply engraved on their hearts. Let them realize and diligently reflect upon the great wisdom, kindness, and bounty God has shown toward the human race, not only by the institution of marriage, but also, and quite as much, by upholding it with sacred laws; still more, in wonderfully raising it to the dignity of a sacrament. By this such an abundant fountain of graces has been opened to those joined in Christian marriage, that they may be able to serve the noble purposes of wedlock for their own welfare and for that of their children, of the community, and also for that of human relationship.

*   *   *

Thus will it come to pass that the faithful will wholeheartedly thank God that they are bound together by His command and led by gentle compulsion to fly as far as possible from every kind of idolatry of the flesh and from the base slavery of the passions. They will, in a great measure, turn and be turned away from these abominable opinions which, to the dishonor of man's dignity, are now spread about in speech and in writing and collected under the title of "perfect marriage," and which indeed would make that perfect marriage nothing better than "depraved marriage," as it has been rightly and truly called.

Such wholesome instruction and religious training in regard to Christian marriage will be quite different from that exaggerated physiological education by means of which, in these times of ours, some reformers of married life make pretense of helping those joined in wedlock, laying much stress on these physiological matters, in which is learned rather the art of sinning in a subtle way than the virtue of living chastely.

*   *   *

Even the very best instruction given by the Church, however, will not alone suffice to bring about once more conformity of marriage to the law of God; something more is needed in addition to the education of the mind, namely a steadfast determination of the will, on the part of husband and wife, to observe the sacred laws of God and of nature in regard to marriage. . . .

*   *   *

. . . For it cannot be denied that the basis of a happy wedlock, and the ruin of an unhappy one, is prepared and set in the souls of boys and girls during the period of childhood and adolescence. There is danger that those who before marriage sought in all things what is theirs, who indulged even their impure desires, will be in the married state what they were before, that they will reap that which they have sown (Gal. 6:9); indeed, within the home there will be sadness, lamentation, mutual contempt, strife, estrangement, weariness of common life, and, worst of all, such parties will find themselves left alone with their own unconquered passions.

Let, then, those who are about to enter on married life, approach that state well disposed and well prepared, so that they will be able, as far as they can, to help each other in sustaining the vicissitudes of life, and yet more in attending to their eternal salvation and in forming the inner man unto the fullness of Christ (Eph. 4:13) [Pius XI, 1930, CC; *SW*, II, 153, 163–167].

When writing about marriage and the Christian family, Pius XII states:

That the family may be established and maintained according to the wise teachings of the Gospel, therefore, the faithful should be frequently exhorted by those who have the directive and teaching functions in the churches, and these are to strive with unremitting care to present to the Lord a perfect people.

For the same reason it is also supremely necessary to see to it that the dogma of the unity and indissolubility of matrimony is known in all its religious importance and sacredly respected by those who are to marry [Pius XII, 1939, *Sertum Laetitiae; CM,* XXXVII, 932].

CHOOSING A MARRIAGE PARTNER

Concerning the choice of a partner in marriage, Pius XI has this to say:

To the proximate preparation of a good married life belongs very specially the care in choosing a partner; on that depends a great deal whether the forthcoming marriage will be happy or not, since one may be to the other either a great help in leading a Christian life, or, a great danger and hindrance. And so that they may not deplore for the rest of their lives the sorrows arising from an indiscreet marriage, those about to enter into wedlock should carefully deliberate in choosing the person with whom henceforward they must live continually: they should, in so deliberating, keep before their minds the thought first of God and of the true religion of Christ, then of themselves, of their partner, of the children to come, as also of human and civil society, for which wedlock is a fountainhead. Let them diligently pray for divine help, so that they make their choice in accordance with Christian prudence, not indeed led by the blind and unrestrained impulse of lust, nor by any desire of riches or other base influence, but by a true and noble love and by a sincere affection for the future partner; and then let them strive in their married life for those ends for which this state was constituted by God. Lastly, let them not omit to ask the prudent advice of their parents with regard to the partner, and let them regard this advice in no light manner, in order that by their mature knowledge and experience of human affairs they may guard against a disastrous choice, and, on the threshold of matrimony, may receive more abundantly the divine blessing of the Fourth Commandment: "Honor thy father and thy mother" — such is the first commandment with a promise — "that it may be well with thee and thou mayest be long-lived upon the earth" (Eph. 6:2–3; Exod. 20:21) [Pius XI, 1930, CC; *SW,* II, 167–168].

PROCREATION OF CHILDREN

Having written about marriage as a sacrament, Leo XIII continues:

Furthermore, the Christian perfection and completeness of marriage are not comprised in those points only which have been mentioned. For, first, there has been vouchsafed to the marriage union a higher and nobler purpose than was ever previously given to it. By the command of Christ, it not only looks to the propagation of the human race, but to the bringing forth of children for the Church, "fellow citizens with the saints, and the domestics of God" (Eph. 2:19); so that "a people might be born and brought up for the worship and religion of the true God and our Saviour Jesus Christ" (Catech. Rom. 8) [Leo XIII, 1880, *Arcanum; SW,* I, 30].

Pope Pius XI, speaking about the blessings of marriage, says:

Thus among the blessings of marriage the child holds the first place. And indeed the Creator of the human race Himself, who in His goodness wished to use men as His helpers in the propagation of life, taught this when, instituting marriage in Paradise, He said to our first parents, and through them to all future spouses: "Increase and multiply, and fill the earth" (Gen. 1:28). As St. Augustine admirably deduces from the words of the holy Apostle St. Paul to Timothy (1 Tim. 5:14) when he says: "The Apostle himself is therefore a witness that marriage is for the sake of generation: 'I wish,' he says, 'young girls to marry.' And, as if someone said to him, 'Why?,' he immediately adds: 'To bear children, to be mothers of families.'"

How great a boon of God this is, and how great a blessing of matrimony is clear from a consideration of man's dignity and of his sublime end. For man surpasses all other visible creatures by the superiority of his rational nature alone. Besides, God wishes men to be born not only that they should live and fill the earth, but much more that they may be worshipers of God, that they may know Him and love Him and finally enjoy Him forever in heaven. This end, since man is raised by God in a marvelous way to the supernatural order, surpasses all that eye hath seen, and ear heard, and all that hath entered into the heart of man (1 Cor. 2:9). From which it is easily seen how great a gift of divine goodness and how remarkable a fruit of marriage are children born by the omnipotent power of God through the co-operation of those bound in wedlock.

But Christian parents must also understand that they are destined not only to propagate and preserve the human race on earth, indeed not only to educate any kind of worshippers of the true God, but children who are to become members of the Church of Christ, to raise up "citizens with the Saints and members of God's household" (Eph. 2:19), that the worshippers of God and our Saviour may daily increase.

*   *   *

. . . This is also expressed succinctly in the Code of Canon Law — "The primary end of marriage is the procreation and the education of children" (*Cod. jur. can.*, c. 1013, 7). [Pius XI, 1930, CC; *SW*, II, 129–131].

Pius XII, addressing newlyweds, said:
. . . The founding of a family is not alone living for oneself, developing one's own physical prowess, one's mind, and one's soul; it is to multiply life, that is to say, it is like rising up and living again, regardless of time and death. . . .

*   *   *

The eternal love of God called the world and humanity into being from nothing; the love of Jesus for His Church generates souls to supernatural life; the love of a Christian husband for his wife participates in these two divine acts because, in accordance with the will of the Creator, man and wife prepare the dwelling of the soul in which the Holy Spirit shall live with His grace. In this manner, through the mission providentially assigned to them, husband and wife are really the collaborators of God and His Christ; their very actions have something of the divine in them, and here too they may be called *divinae consortes* naturae [Pius XII, 1940, *Scritti e Discorsi,* II; *The Pope Speaks to Newlyweds,* pp. 19, 56].

Speaking to Italian midwives, Pius XII said:
The truth is that matrimony as a natural institution, by virtue of the will of the Creator, does not have as its primary, intimate end the personal improvement of the couples concerned but the procreation and the education of new life. The other ends though also connected with nature are not in the same rank as the first, still less are they superior to it. They are subordinated to it. This holds true for every marriage, even if it bear no fruit, just as it can be said that every eye is made for seeing although in certain abnormal cases, because of special internal and external conditions, it will never be able to see.

Some years ago (March 10, 1944) with the precise aim of putting an end to all these uncertainties and errors that threatened to spread mistakes about matrimony and the mutual relation of its ends, We ourselves made a statement on the order of these ends. We indicated what the inner structure of the natural disposition reveals, what is the heritage of Christian tradition, what the Sovereign Pontiffs have frequently taught, and what is established in proper form by the Code of Canon Law (Canon 1013 para I). A few years later, to correct conflicting opinions, the Holy See issued a public decree stating that the opinion of certain recent authors could not be admitted, authors who denied that the primary end of matrimony was the procreation and rearing of children or taught that the secondary ends of marriage are not subordinated to the primary end but of equal importance and independent of it (*S.C.C. Officii,* April 1, 1944; *Acta Ap. Sedis,* Vol. 36, 1944, p. 103) [Pius XII, 1951, *Apostolate of the Midwife; CM,* L, 60].

MARRIED PERSONS HELD TO FULFILLMENT OF A POSITIVE WORK

Pope Pius XII says:
The reason for this is that marriage obliges to a state of life

which, while conferring certain rights also imposes the fulfillment of a positive work in regard to the married state itself. In such a case, one can apply the general principle that a positive fulfillment may be omitted when serious reasons, independent from the good will of those obliged by it, show that this action is not opportune, or prove that a similar demand cannot reasonably be made of human nature.

The marriage contract which confers upon husband and wife the right to satisfy the inclinations of nature, sets them up in a certain state of life, the married state. But upon couples who perform the act peculiar to their state, nature and the Creator impose the function of helping the conservation of the human race. The characteristic activity which gives their state its value is the bonum prolis ("the good of the offspring"). The individual and society, the people and the state, the Church itself depend for their existence in the order established by God on fruitful marriage. Therefore, to embrace the married state, continuously to make use of the faculty proper to it and lawful in it alone, and, on the other hand, to withdraw always and deliberately with no serious reason from its primary obligation, would be a sin against the very meaning of conjugal life [Pius XII, 1951, *Apostolate of the Midwife; CM, L, 57*].

SEXUAL INTERCOURSE LAWFUL IN MARRIAGE

Speaking of the duties of parents, Pius XI writes:

Nor must We omit to remark, in fine, that since the duty entrusted to parents for the good of their children is of such a truly high dignity and of such great importance, every use of the faculty given by God for the procreation of new life is the right and privilege of the married state alone, by the law of God and of nature, and must be confined absolutely within the sacred limits of that state [Pius XI, 1930, CC; *SW*, II, 131].

Concerning the sexual act, Pius XII states:

Nevertheless, even here couples must know how to restrict themselves within the limits of moderation. As in eating and drinking, so in the sexual act, they must not abandon themselves without restraint to the impulse of the senses. The right norm therefore is this: The use of the natural inclination to generate is lawful only in matrimony, in the service of and according to the order of the ends of marriage. From this it follows that only in marriage, and by observing this rule, the desire for and the fruit of this pleasure and satisfaction are lawful. . . . [Pius XII, 1951, *Apostolate of the Midwife; CM*, L, 62].

MARRIED COUPLES MAY SEEK AND ENJOY SEX PLEASURE

In defense of human dignity in the use of the generative inclination, Pius XII writes:

The Creator Who in His goodness and wisdom has willed to conserve and propagate the human race through the instrumentality of man and woman by uniting them in marriage has ordained also that in performing this function, husband and wife should experience pleasure and happiness both in body and soul. In seeking and enjoying this pleasure, therefore, couples do nothing wrong. They accept that which the Creator has given them [Pius XII, 1951, *Apostolate of the Midwife; CM*, L, 62].

OBLIGATION TO CONTROL SEX PASSIONS

Pius XI writes that sex passions can be controlled by submitting to God's will.

Wherefore, since the chief obstacle to this study is the power of unbridled lust, which indeed is the most potent cause of sinning against the sacred laws of matrimony, and since man cannot hold in check his passions, unless he first subject himself to God, this must be his primary endeavor, in accordance with the plan divinely ordained. For it is a sacred ordinance that whoever shall have first subjected himself to God will, by the aid of divine grace, be glad to subject to himself his own passions and concupiscence; while he who is a rebel against God will, to his sorrow, experience within himself the violent rebellion of his worst passions [Pius XI, 1930, CC; *SW*, II, 160].

Concerning the obligation to dominate the passions, Pius XII writes:

Transgression of this rule is as old as original sin. But in our times there is the risk of losing sight of the basic principle. At present it is the custom to maintain in word and writing (and some Catholics do it too) the necessary autonomy, the proper end, and the proper value of sexuality and its performance independently of the object of procreation. People want to re-examine and find a new rule for the order established by God. They do not want to admit any other check on the manner of satisfying instinct than observing the essence of the instinctive act. Thus, for the moral obligation to dominate the passions there is substituted license to follow blindly and without restraint the caprices and impulses of nature, a line of conduct which sooner or later can but lead to the damage of man's morals, conscience, and dignity.

If nature had aimed exclusively or even primarily at a mutual gift and mutual possession of couples for pleasure, if it had ordained that act solely to make their personal experience happy in the highest degree and not to stimulate them in the service of life, then the Creator would have adopted another plan in the formation and constitution of the natural act. But this act is completely subordinated to and ordered in accordance with the sole great law of "generatio et educatio prolis" ("the education and generation of offspring"), the fulfilling of the primary end of matrimony as the origin and source of life.

Unfortunately, never-ending waves of hedonism sweep over the world and threaten to drown all married life in the rising flood of thoughts, desires, and acts, not without grave dangers and serious damage to the primary duty of man and wife.

Too often this anti-Christian hedonism does not blush to raise this theory to a doctrine by inculcating the desire to intensify continually enjoyment in the preparation and carrying out of the conjugal union, as though in matrimonial relations the whole moral law were reduced to a regular completion of the act itself and as though all the rest, no matter how accomplished, remained justified in the pouring out of mutual affection, sanctified by the sacrament of matrimony. . . .

*   *   *

. . . The seriousness and sanctity of the Christian moral law do not admit unbridled satisfaction of the sexual instinct tending merely to pleasure and enjoyment. The moral law does not allow man with his reason to let himself be dominated to that point, be it a question of the substance or the circumstances of the act [Pius XII, 1951, *Apostolate of the Midwife; CM,* L, 62–63].

LAW GOVERNING CONJUGAL RELATIONS

Regarding conjugal relations, the traditional Christian teaching must be upheld, says Pius XI.

Since, therefore, openly departing from the uninterrupted Christian tradition some recently have judged it possible solemnly to declare another doctrine regarding this question, the Catholic Church, to whom God has entrusted the defense of the integrity and purity of morals, standing erect in the midst of the moral ruin which surrounds her, that so she may preserve the chastity of the nuptial union from being defiled by this foul stain, raises her voice in token of her divine ambassadorship and through Our mouth proclaims anew: any use whatsoever of matrimony exercised in such a way that the act is deliberately frustrated in its natural power to generate life is an offense against the law of God and of nature, and those who indulge in such are branded with the guilt of a grave sin [Pius XI, 1930, CC; *SW,* II, 144].

Pius XII restates the teaching of the Church concerning conjugal relations, and asserts that the Church's teaching can never be changed.

In his Encyclical *Casti Connubii* of December 31, 1930, Our predecessor, Pius XI, of happy memory, solemnly restated the basic law of the conjugal act and conjugal relations. "Every attempt on the part of the married couple during the conjugal act or during the development of its natural consequences, to deprive it of its inherent power and to hinder the procreation of a new life is immoral. No 'indication' or need can change an action that is intrinsically immoral into an action that is moral and lawful" (Acta Ap. Sedis, Vol. 22, p. 559 *seq.*).

This prescription holds good today just as much as it did yesterday. It will hold tomorrow and always, for it is not a mere precept of human right but the expression of a natural and Divine law [Pius XII, 1951, *Apostolate of the Midwife; CM, L,* 55].

USE OF THE STERILE PERIOD

Pius XI states that sexual intercourse is lawful during the sterile period.

. . . Nor are those considered as acting against nature who in the married state use their right in the proper manner although on account of natural reasons either of time or of certain defect, new life cannot be brought forth. For in matrimony as well as in the use of the matrimonial rights there are also secondary ends, such as mutual aid, the cultivating of mutual love, and the quieting of concupiscence which husband and wife are not forbidden to consider so long as these are subordinated to the primary end and so long as the intrinsic nature of the act is preserved [Pius XI, 1930, CC; *SW,* II, 145].

About the sterile period, Pius XII writes:

Then, there is the serious question today as to whether and how far the obligation of ready disposition to serve motherhood can be reconciled with the ever more widely diffused recourse to the periods of natural sterility (the so-called agenetic periods of the woman) which seems to be a clear expression of the will contrary to that disposition.

. . . Here it is the Church that is the competent judge.

There are two hypotheses to be considered. If the carrying out of this theory means nothing more than that the couple can make use of their matrimonial rights on the days of natural sterility too, there is nothing against it, for by so doing they neither hinder nor injure in any way the consummation of the natural act and its further natural consequences. It is in this respect that the application of the theory of which we have spoken differs from the abuse already mentioned which is a perversion of the act itself. If, however, it is a further question — that is, of permitting the conjugal act on those days exclusively — then the conduct of the married couple must be examined more closely.

Here two other hypotheses present themselves to us. If at the time of marriage at least one of the couple intended to restrict the marriage right, not merely its use, to the sterile periods, in such a way that at other times the second party would not even have the right to demand the act, this would imply an essential defect in the consent to marriage, which would carry with it invalidity of the marriage itself, because the right deriving from the contract of marriage is a permanent, uninterrupted and not intermittent right of each of the parties, one to the other.

On the other hand, if the act be limited to the sterile periods insofar as the mere use and not the right is concerned, there is no question about the validity of the marriage. Nevertheless, the moral licitness of such conduct on the part of the couple would have to be approved or denied according as to whether or not the intention of observing those periods constantly was based on sufficient and secure moral grounds. The mere fact that the couple do not offend the nature of the act and are prepared to accept and bring up the child which in spite of their precautions came into the world would not be sufficient in itself to guarantee the rectitude of intention and the unobjectionable morality of the motives themselves [Pius XII, 1951, *Apostolate of the Midwife; CM,* L, 56–57].

SERIOUS REASONS ARE NECESSARY TO RESTRICT CONJUGAL RELATIONS TO THE STERILE PERIOD

Pius XII states that conjugal relations may be restricted to the sterile periods for grave reasons.

There are serious motives, such as those often mentioned in the so-called medical, eugenic, economic, and social "indications," that can exempt for a long time, perhaps even the whole duration of the marriage, from the positive and obligatory carrying out of the act. From this it follows that observing the non-fertile periods alone can be lawful only under a moral aspect. Under the conditions mentioned it really is so. But if, according to a rational and just judgment, there are no similar grave reasons of a personal nature or deriving from external circumstances, then the determination to avoid habitually the fecundity of the union while at the same time to continue fully satisfying their sensuality, can be derived only from a false appreciation of life and from reasons having nothing to do with proper ethical laws [Pius XII, 1951, *Apostolate of the Midwife; CM*, L, 57].

Speaking about regulating the offspring, Pius XII says:
. . . the Church knows how to consider with sympathy and understanding the real difficulties of the married state in our day. Therefore, in Our late allocution on conjugal morality, We affirmed the legitimacy and, at the same time, the limits — in truth very wide — of a regulation of offspring, which, unlike so-called "birth control," is compatible with the law of God. One may even hope (but in this matter the Church naturally leaves the judgment to medical science) that science will succeed in providing this licit method with a sufficiently secure basis, and the most recent information seems to confirm such a hope [Pius XII, 1952, *Morality in Marriage; CM*, L, 311].

IF RISK OF MOTHERHOOD IS GRAVE, COMPLETE ABSTINENCE MUST BE PRACTICED

Concerning this, Pius XII said to the Italian Catholic Union of Midwives:
Now you might insist observing, perhaps, that in the exercise of your profession you sometimes come across very delicate cases in which the risk of motherhood cannot be run or must be avoided completely, and in which, on the other hand, observing the sterile periods either does not give sufficient security or has to

be abandoned for other reasons. And then you ask how one can still speak of an apostolate in the service of maternity.

If in your reliable and experienced judgment, conditions absolutely demand a "no" (that is that maternity must be excluded), it would be a mistake and a wrong to impose or counsel a "yes." Here we are dealing with concrete facts, with a medical not theological question, one, therefore, which you are competent to handle. But in such cases couples do not ask you for a medical answer, which is necessarily negative, but for approval of a "technique" of the conjugal act which insures them against the risk of motherhood. Here is another occasion on which you are called to exercise your apostolate, insofar as you do not leave any doubt that even in such extreme cases every preventive step and every direct attempt upon the life and development of the germ is in conscience prohibited and excluded, and that there is but one way open, that of complete abstinence from every complete exercise of the natural faculty. Here your apostolate obliges you to clear, sure judgment and calm firmness [Pius XII, 1951, *Apostolate of the Midwife; CM,* L, 58].

COMPLETE SEXUAL ABSTINENCE IS POSSIBLE FOR MARRIED COUPLES

Pius XI states that God's laws can be observed under all circumstances.

. . . No difficulty can arise that justifies the putting aside of the law of God which forbids all acts intrinsically evil. There is no possible circumstance in which husband and wife cannot, strengthened by the grace of God, fulfill faithfully their duties and preserve in wedlock their chastity unspotted. This truth of Christian faith is expressed by the teaching of the Council of Trent. "Let no one be so rash as to assert that which the Fathers of the Council have placed under anathema, namely, that there are precepts of God impossible for the just to observe. God does not ask the impossible, but by His commands, instructs you to do what you are able, to pray for what you are not able that He may help you" (Conc. Trid., Sess. vi, c. II).

This same doctrine was again solemnly repeated and confirmed by the Church in the condemnation of the Jansenist heresy which dared to utter this blasphemy against the goodness of God: "Some precepts of God are, when one considers the powers which man possesses, impossible of fulfillment even to the just who wish to keep the law and strive to do so; grace is lacking whereby these laws could be fulfilled" (Apost. Const., *Cum Occasione,* May 31, 1653, prop. I) [Pius XI, 1930, CC; *SW*, II, 145–146].

Pius XII says even though some hold that such heroism is impossible, it is possible for married couples to abstain from sex relations for a long time.

But it will be objected that such abstinence is impossible, that such heroism cannot be attained. Today you will hear and read this objection on all sides, even from those who on account of their duty and ability should be able to judge very differently. The following argument is brought forward as a proof: "No one is obliged to do the impossible and no reasonable legislator, it is assumed, wishes by his law to oblige people to do the impossible. But, for married couples long-term abstinence is impossible. Therefore they are not obliged to abstain. The Divine law cannot mean this."

Thus, from partly true premises a false conclusion is deduced. In order to convince yourself of this, invert the steps of the argument. God does not oblige people to do the impossible. But God obliges married people to abstain, if their union cannot be fulfilled according to the laws of nature. Therefore, in this case abstinence is possible. In confirmation of this argument we have the Council of Trent which, in its chapter on the observance, necessary and possible, of the commandments teaches us that, as St. Augustine said, "God does not command impossible things, but when He commands He warns us to do what can be done and to ask what cannot and gives you help so that you can" (Conc. Trid. Sess. 6, Cap. II. Denzinger, n. 804. S. August.,

De natura et gratis, Cap. 43, n. 50. Migne, *P.L.,* vol. 44, col. 271).

Therefore, do not allow yourselves to be confused in the practice of your profession and your apostolate by all this talk about impossibility, either as regards your own inner judgment or in what concerns your outward conduct. Never do anything contrary to the law of God and your consciences as Christians. It is wronging men and women of our times to deem them incapable of continuous heroism. Today, for many reasons — perhaps with the goad of hard necessity or even sometimes in the service of injustice — heroism is exercised to a degree and to an extent which would have been thought impossible in days gone by. Why, then, should this heroism, if the circumstances really demand it, stop at the borders established by the passions and inclinations of nature? The answer is clear. The man who does not want to master himself is incapable of so doing. He who believes he can do so, counting merely on his own strength without seeking sincerely and perseveringly help from God, will remain miserably disillusioned [Pius XII, 1951, *Apostolate of the Midwife; CM,* L, 58–59].

ARTIFICIAL BIRTH CONTROL

About the evils opposed to the benefits of matrimony, Pius XI writes:

First consideration is due to the offspring, which many have the boldness to call the disagreeable burden of matrimony. This, they say, is to be carefully avoided by married people, not through virtuous continence (which Christian law permits in matrimony when both parties consent), but by frustrating the marriage act. Some justify this criminal abuse on the ground that they are weary of children and wish to gratify their desires without their consequent burden. Others say that they cannot on the one hand remain continent, nor on the other can they have children, because of the difficulties whether on the part of the mother or on the part of family circumstances.

But no reason, however grave, can be put forward by which

anything intrinsically against nature may become conformable to nature and morally good. Since, therefore, the conjugal act is destined primarily by nature for the begetting of children, those who in exercising it deliberately frustrate its natural power and purpose sin against nature and commit a deed which is shameful and intrinsically vicious.

Small wonder, therefore, if Holy Writ bears witness that the Divine Majesty regards with greatest detestation this horrible crime and at times has punished it with death. As St. Augustine notes, "Intercourse even with one's legitimate wife is unlawful and wicked where the conception of the offspring is prevented. Onan, the son of Juda, did this and the Lord killed him for it."

*   *   *

Holy Church knows well that not infrequently one of the parties is sinned against rather than sinning, when for a grave cause he or she reluctantly allows the perversion of the right order. In such a case, there is no sin, provided that, mindful of the law of charity, he or she does not neglect to seek to dissuade and to deter the partner from sin . . . [Pius XI, 1930, CC; *SW*, II, 143–145].

Pope Pius XII, addressing newlyweds on their obligations to found a family, said:

Unhappy the married couple who have not understood and felt the pleasure of this hope! And unhappier still and guilty too they who, in opposition to the laws of the Creator, have restricted or closed the door to the family (i.e., practice birth control). . . .

*   *   *

. . . You also, my dear newlyweds, should give yourselves unreservedly to God in the new state of life to which you have been called. Beginning with this day, take upon yourselves seriously the grave obligations it imposes upon you. Guard yourselves against continuing a life which was perhaps thoughtless and frivolous: lazy and dissolute for the young men, frivolous and self-indulgent for the young women. Expend all your energies upon the duties of your new state. The time has passed when little girls were often married without understanding the meaning of marriage; but unfortunately the time is still with us when many young married people believe they can in the beginning, permit themselves a period of moral liberty and enjoy their rights without a thought for their duties. This is a serious mistake which brings down upon it the wrath of God. It is the source of even temporal unhappiness, whose consequences should cause everyone to be afraid. A duty that one will not recognize or that he despises, is always put off so long that one ends by almost forgetting it, and with it goes the happiness that its courageous performance would have brought. And when one does remember and is sorry, he sometimes arrives at the sad truth that it is too late. A couple who has been unfaithful to its mission, can only shrivel up, without hope, in the desert of its sterile selfishness [Pius XII, 1940, *Scritti e Discorsi,* II; *The Holy Father Speaks to Newlyweds,* pp. 19, 43].

EUGENICS

Concerning the morality of eugenics, Pius XI writes:
. . . That pernicious practice must be condemned which closely touches upon the natural right of man to enter matrimony but affects also in a real way the welfare of the offspring. For there are some who, oversolicitous for the cause of "eugenics," not only give salutary counsel for more certainly procuring the strength and health of the future child — which, indeed, is not contrary to right reason — but put "eugenics" before aims of a higher order. By public authority they wish to forbid marriage to all those who, even though naturally fit for marriage, are regarded, in accordance with the norms and conjectures of their investigations, as persons who through hereditary transmission would bring forth defective offspring. And more, they wish to legislate to deprive these of that natural faculty by medical action, despite their unwillingness. And this they propose to do, not as an infliction of grave punishment under the authority of the state for a crime committed, nor to prevent future crimes by

guilty persons, but against every right and good they wish the civil authority to arrogate to itself a power over a faculty which it never had and never can legitimately possess.

Those who act in this way are at fault in losing sight of the fact that the family is more sacred than the state and that men are begotten not for the earth and for time, but for heaven and eternity. Although often these individuals are to be dissuaded from entering into matrimony, certainly it is wrong to brand men with the stigma of crime because they contract marriage, on the ground that, despite the fact that they are in every respect capable of matrimony, they will give birth only to defective children, even though they use all care and diligence [Pius XI, 1930, CC; *SW,* II, 148].

STERILIZATION

Pius XI states that sterilization can become a grave violation of the moral law.

Public magistrates have no direct power over the bodies of their subjects; therefore, where no crime has taken place and there is no cause present for grave punishment, they can never directly harm, or tamper with the integrity of the body, either for the reasons of eugenics or for any other reason. St. Thomas teaches this when, inquiring whether human judges for the sake of preventing future evils can inflict punishment, he admits that the power indeed exists as regards certain other forms of evil, but justly and properly denies it as regards the maiming of the body. "No one who is guiltless may be punished by a human tribunal either by flogging to death, or mutilation, or by beating" (2a, 2ae, q. 108, a. 4 ad 2).

Furthermore, Christian doctrine establishes, and the light of human reason makes it most clear, that private individuals have no other power over the members of their bodies than that which pertains to their natural ends; and they are not free to destroy or mutilate their members, or in any other way render themselves unfit for their natural functions, except when no other provision can be made for the good of the whole body [Pius XI, 1930, CC; *SW*, II, 148–149].

Pius XII indicates the immorality of sterilization. He says:

It would be very much more than a mere lack of readiness in the service of life if the man's attempt affected not just a single act but the organism itself, in order to sterilize and deprive it of the faculty of procreating a new life. In this case, too, you have, in the teaching of the Church, a clear rule for your inward and outward conduct. Direct sterilization, that which aims at making procreation impossible as both means and end, is a grave violation of the moral law, and therefore illicit. Even public authority has no right to permit it under the pretext of any "indication" whatsoever, and still less to prescribe it or to have it carried out to the harm of the innocent. This principle has been already stated in the Encyclical of Pius XI which we have quoted (pp. 564–565). Therefore, ten years ago, when sterilization came to be more widely applied, the Holy See found itself in need of stating expressly and publicly that direct sterilization, either permanent or temporary, of man or of woman, is illegal by virtue of the natural law from which, as you are aware, the Church has no power to dispense. . . .

Use all your strength therefore in opposing these perverse tendencies and refuse to co-operate with them [Pius XII, 1951, *Apostolate of the Midwife; CM*, L, 55–56].

ABORTION

Concerning this immoral practice, Pius XI writes:

. . . Another very grave crime is to be noted, Venerable Brethren, which regards the taking of the life of the offspring hidden in the mother's womb. Some wish it to be allowed and left to the will of the father or the mother; others say it is unlawful unless there are weighty reasons which they call by the name of medical, social, or eugenic "indication." Because this matter falls under the penal laws of the state by which the destruction of the offspring begotten but unborn is forbidden, these people demand that the "indication," which in one form or another they defend, be recognized as such by the public law and in no way penalized. There are those, moreover, who ask that the public authorities provide aid for these death-dealing operations, a thing which, sad to say, everyone knows is of very frequent occurrence in some places.

As to the "medical and therapeutic indication" to which, using their own words, we have made reference, Venerable Brethren, however much we may pity the mother whose health and even life is gravely imperiled in the performance of the duty allotted to her by nature, nevertheless what could ever be a sufficient reason for excusing in any way the direct murder of the innocent? This is precisely what we are dealing with here. Whether inflicted upon the mother or upon the child, it is against the precept of God and the law of nature: "Thou shalt not kill": The life of each is equally sacred, and no one has the power, not even the public authority, to destroy it. It is of no use to appeal to the right of taking away life, for here it is a question of the innocent, whereas that right has regard only to the guilty. Nor is there question here of defense by bloodshed against an unjust aggressor (for who would call an innocent child an unjust aggressor?). Again there is no question here of what is called the "law of extreme necessity" which could even extend to the direct killing of the innocent. Upright and skillful doctors strive most praiseworthily to guard and preserve the lives of both mother and child; on the contrary, those show themselves most unworthy of the noble medical profession who encompass the death of one or the other, through a pretense of practising medicine or through motives of misguided pity.

All of which agrees with the stern words of the Bishop of Hippo in denouncing those wicked parents who seek to remain childless, and failing in this, are not ashamed to put their offspring to death: "Sometimes this lustful cruelty or cruel lust goes so far as to seek to procure a baneful sterility, if this fails the foetus conceived in the womb is in one way or another smothered or evacuated, in the desire to destroy the offspring before it has life, or if it already lives in the womb, to kill it before it is born. If both man and woman are party to such practices they are not spouses at all; and if from the first they have carried on thus they have come together not for honest wedlock, but for impure gratification; if both are not party to these deeds, I make bold to say that either the one makes herself a mistress of the husband, or the other simply the paramour of his wife" (*De Nupt. et Concup.*, xv).

What is asserted in favor of the social and eugenic "indication" may and must be accepted, provided lawful and upright methods are employed within the proper limits; but to wish to put forward reasons based upon them for the killing of the innocent is unthinkable and contrary to the divine precept promulgated in the words of the Apostle: Evil is not to be done that good may come of it (Rom. 3:8).

Those who hold the reins of government should not forget that it is the duty of public authority by appropriate laws and sanctions to defend the lives of the innocent, and this all the more so since those whose lives are endangered and assailed cannot defend themselves. Among whom we must mention in the first place infants hidden in the mother's womb. And if the public magistrates not only do not defend them, but by their law and ordinances betray them to death at the hands of doctors or of others, let them remember that God is the Judge and Avenger of the innocent blood which cries from earth to heaven (Gen. 4:10) [Pius XI, 1930, CC; *SW*, II, 146–148].

In defense of the unborn child, Pius XII writes:

. . . Now the infant is "man," even though it be not yet born, to the same degree and through the same title as the mother.

Every human being, even the infant in the maternal womb, has the right to life immediately from God, not from the parents or any human society or authority. Therefore there is no man, no human authority, no science, no medical, eugenic, social, economic, or moral "indication," that can show or give a valid juridical title for direct deliberate disposition concerning an innocent human life — which is to say, a disposition that aims at its destruction either as an end in itself or as the means of attaining another end that is perhaps in no way illicit in itself.

Thus, for example, to save the life of the mother is a most noble end, but the direct killing of the child as a means to this end is not licit. The direct destruction of what they call "worthless life" born or unborn, practiced a few years ago on many occasions, can be justified in no way. . . .

*   *   *

. . . And when necessary and you are able to do so, you must protect the defenseless and still hidden life of the child supporting your action with the force of the Divine Commandment "Thou shalt not kill" (Exod. 20:13) . . . [Pius XII, 1951, *Apostolate of the Midwife; CM*, L, 51–52].

. . . Any direct attempt on an innocent human life as a means to an end — in this case to the end of saving another life — is unlawful.

Innocent human life, in whatsoever condition it is found, is withdrawn, from the very first moment of its existence, from any direct deliberate attack. This is a fundamental right of the human person, which is of general value in the Christian conception of life; hence as valid for the life still hidden within the womb of the mother, as for the life already born and developing outside of her; as much opposed to direct abortion as to the direct killing of the child before, during or after its birth. Whatever foundation there may be for the distinction between these various phases of the development of life that is born or still unborn, in profane and ecclesiastical law, and as regards certain civil and penal consequences, all these cases involve a grave and unlawful attack upon the inviolability of human life.

This principle holds good both for the life of the child as well as for that of the mother. Never and in no case has the Church taught that the life of the child must be preferred to that of the mother. It is erroneous to put the question with this alternative: either the life of the child or that of the mother. No, neither the life of the mother nor that of the child can be subjected to an act of direct suppression. In the one case as in the other, there can be but one obligation: to make every effort to save the lives of both . . . (cf. Pius XI, Encycl. *Casti Connubii,* Dec. 31, 1930 — *Acta Ap. Sedis,* vol. 22, p. 562–563).

It is one of the finest and most noble aspirations of the medical profession to search for ever new ways of ensuring the life of both. But if, notwithstanding all the progress of science, there still remain, and will remain in the future, cases in which one must reckon with the death of the mother, when it is the mother's wish to bring to birth the life that is within her, and not to destroy it in violation of the command of God: Thou shalt not kill! — nothing else remains for the man, who will make every effort right up to the last moment to help and save, but to bow respectfully before the laws of nature and the dispositions of Divine Providence.

But — it is objected — the life of the mother, especially the mother of a large family, is of incomparably greater value than that of a child not yet born. The application of the theory of the equivalation of values to the case which occupies Us has already been accepted in juridical discussions. The reply to this harrowing objection is not difficult. The inviolability of the life of an innocent human being does not depend on its greater or lesser value. It is already more than ten years since the Church formally condemned the killing of life considered to be "without value"; and whosoever knows the sad events that preceded and provoked that condemnation, whosoever is able to weigh up the direful consequences that would result, if one were to try to measure the inviolability of innocent life according to its value, knows well how to appreciate the motives that determined that disposition.

Besides, who can judge with certainty which of the two lives is in fact the more precious? Who can know what path that child will follow and to what heights of achievement and perfection he may reach? Two greatnesses are being compared here, one of them being an unknown quantity.

In this regard We wish to cite an example which may perhaps

be already known to some of you but which notwithstanding that fact loses none of its suggestiveness. It goes back to the year 1905. At that time there was a young lady of noble birth and of still nobler sentiments, but who was frail and of delicate constitution. As a young girl she had been ill with a slight apical pleurisy, which seemed cured; when, however, having contracted a happy marriage, she felt a new life springing in her womb, she soon became aware of a peculiar physical indisposition, which alarmed the two able doctors who were attending her with every care and solicitude. The old apical trouble, the cicatrized lesion had become active again; in their opinion there was no time to lose; if the gentle lady was to be saved, a therapeutic abortion would have to be provoked without the least delay.

The husband also realized the gravity of the case and signified his consent to the distressful act. But when the midwife in attendance duly made known the decision of the doctors and beseeched her to defer to their opinion, she replied with firm voice: "I thank you for your merciful advice; but I cannot suppress the life of my child! I cannot, I cannot! I feel it already throbbing in my womb; it has the right to live; it comes from God and should know God as to love and enjoy Him."

Her husband also entreated, supplicated and implored her; she remained inflexible and quietly awaited the event. A baby girl was regularly born; but, immediately after, the health of the mother began to get worse. The pulmonary lesion spread; the deterioration became progressive. Two months later she was at the limit of her forces; she once again saw her little child who was growing healthily under the care of a robust nurse; her lips broke into a sweet smile and she passed away peacefully.

Many years went by. In a religious institute a young Sister might be particularly noticed, totally dedicated to the care and education of abandoned children, bending over sick little ones, with eyes full of maternal love, as if to give them life. It was she, the daughter of the sacrifice, who now with her generous heart was doing so much good among abandoned children. The heroism of her fearless mother had not been in vain! (Cfr. Andrea Majocchi, *Tra Bistori o Forbici* (*With Surgical Knives and Scissors*), 1940, p. 21 etc.).

But We ask: Is it possible that Christian sensibility, even also purely human sensibility, has been dulled to the point that it cannot any longer appreciate the sublime holocaust of the mother and the visible action of divine Providence, which brought forth such a splendid fruit from that holocaust?

On purpose We have always used the expression "direct attempt on the life of an innocent person," "direct killing." Because if, for example, the saving of the life of the future mother, independently of her pregnant state, should urgently require a surgical act or other therapeutic treatment which would have as an accessory consequence, in no way desired nor intended but inevitable, the death of the fetus, such act could no longer be called a direct attempt on an innocent life. Under these conditions the operation can be licit, like other similar medical interventions, granted always that a good of high worth is concerned, such as life, and that it is not possible to postpone the operation until after the birth of the child, nor to have recourse to other efficacious remedies [Pius XII, 1952, *Morality in Marriage; CM*, L, 308–310].

EUTHANASIA

Addressing the Congress of the International Union of Catholic Women's Leagues, Rome, Italy, Pope Pius XII said:

. . . It is not enough to be good, tender, generous; one must also be wise and strong. The indulgent weakness of parents blinds them, to the detriment of their children. In the social order, a similar sentimentality blinds the mind and leads it to hold monstrous theories and to extol immoral and fatal practices. Is it not such false pity which claims to justify euthanasia and to remove from man purifying and meritorious suffering, not by a charitable and praiseworthy help but by death, as if one were

dealing with an irrational animal without immortality? . . .
[Pius XII, 1947, *Papal Directives for the Woman of Today;
Catholic Action*, XXX, 18].

To the Italian Catholic Union of Midwives, Pius XII said:
. . . The direct destruction of what they call "worthless life"
born or unborn, practiced a few years ago on many occasions,
can be justified in no way. For this reason, when this practice
began, the Church formally declared that the killing, even by
order of public authority, of those who although innocent are not
only useless to the nation on account of physical or psychic
defects but also a burden upon it, is contrary to positive natural
and divine right and therefore, illegal (Dec. Holy Office, 2 Dec.,
1940 — *Acta Apos. Sedis,* Vol. 32, 1940, pp. 553–554). The life
of an innocent person is untouchable. Any direct attempt or ag-
gression against it is a violation of one of the basic laws without
which men cannot live together in safety. There is no need for
us to go into details regarding the significance and weight of
this basic law as far as your profession is concerned. But remember that the law of God rises unshakable above all human laws,
above all "indications" . . . [Pius XII, 1951, *Apostolate of the
Midwife; CM,* L, 51].

ARTIFICIAL INSEMINATION

*Speaking to the Fourth International Convention of Catholic
Doctors, Pius XII said:*
The practice of artificial insemination, when it is applied to
man, cannot be considered exclusively, nor even principally, from
the biological and medical viewpoint while leaving aside the viewpoint of morality and law.

Artificial insemination outside marriage is to be condemned
purely and simply as immoral.

In fact, the natural law and the positive Divine Law are such
that the procreation of new life may only be the fruit of marriage . . . marriage alone provides for the good and education
of the offspring. Consequently, there is no possibility of any

divergence of opinion among Catholics regarding the condemnation of artificial insemination outside marriage. A child conceived in such condition is, by that fact alone, illegitimate.

Artificial insemination in marriage with the use of an active element from a third person is equally immoral and as such is to be rejected summarily. Only the marriage partners have mutual rights over their bodies for the procreation of a new life and these are exclusive, non-transferable and inalienable rights. So it must be, out of consideration for the child.

*   *   *

With regard to the lawfulness of artificial insemination in marriage, it is sufficient for us at present to recall the principles of the natural law: the simple fact that the desired result is obtained by this means does not justify the employment of the method itself; nor does the desire of the marriage partners — most legitimate in itself — to have a child, suffice to prove the lawfulness of a recourse to artificial insemination for the fulfilment of that desire.

It would be false to believe that the possibility of a recourse to that method would render a marriage valid between two persons who are unfitted to contract a marriage because of the impediment of impotency.

Moreover, it is superfluous to indicate that the active element can never be lawfully attained by acts that are contrary to nature.

*   *   *

. . . Artificial insemination is something which must not just be regarded with extreme reserve, but must be utterly rejected . . . [Pius XII, 1949, *To Catholic Doctors; CM*, XLVIII, 252–253].

To the Italian Catholic Union of Midwives, Pius XII said:

To reduce cohabitation and the conjugal act to a simple organic function for the transmission of seed would be converting the home, the sanctuary of the family, into a mere biological laboratory. In our address of September 29, 1949, to the International Congress of Catholic Doctors, we formally excluded artificial insemination from marriage. In its natural structure, the conjugal act is a personal action, a simultaneous and immediate co-operation on the part of the husband and wife which by the very nature of the agents and the propriety of the act is the expression of the mutual gift which according to Holy Scripture brings about union "in one flesh only."

This is something much more than the union of two seeds which may be brought about even artificially, without the natural action of husband and wife. The conjugal act, ordained and willed by nature is a personal act of co-operation, the right to which husband and wife give each other when they marry.

Therefore, when this act, in its natural form, is from the beginning and permanently impossible, the end and object of the marriage contract suffer from an essential defect. This is what we said on that occasion: "Do not forget. Solely the procreation of a new life according to the will and plan of the Creator brings with it in a wonderful degree of perfection, the accomplishment of the ends intended. At the same time it is in conformity with the corporal and spiritual nature and the dignity of husband and wife, with the normal and happy development of the child" (*Acta Ap. Sedis,* Vol. 41, 1949, p. 560) [Pius XII, 1951, *Apostolate of the Midwife; CM,* L, 61].

PARENTHOOD

Pius XI reminds husband and wife to accept their children with joy and gratitude from the hand of God.

. . . A true Christian mother . . . will indeed understand with a sense of deep consolation that of her the words of our Saviour were spoken: "A woman . . . when she hath brought forth the child she no longer remembers the anguish for her joy that a man is born into the world" (John 16:21); and proving herself superior to all the pains and cares and solicitudes of her maternal office, with a more just and holy joy than that of the Roman matron, the mother of the Gracchi, she will rejoice in the Lord, crowned as it were with the glory of her offspring. Both husband and wife, however, receiving these children with joy and gratitude from the hand of God, will regard them as a talent committed to their charge by God, not only to be employed for their own advantage or for that of an earthly commonwealth, but to be restored to God with interest on the day of reckoning [Pius XI, 1930, CC; *SW*, II, 130].

Speaking to newlyweds, Pius XII remarked:

. . . May you see in the dear little ones which will come, we hope, to bring happiness to your home before becoming the strength of your maturity and the prop of your old age, not alone the tender limbs, the sweet smile, the eyes in which will be reflected your countenance and even the deepest affections of your heart, but above all, and before all, the soul created by God, a precious charge confided to you by the Divine Goodness. . . .

* * *

. . . The children are the living image and, so to speak, the resurrection of their ancestors, who thus reach from one generation to the next. In them you will see live and act before you, often with the same features and the same traditions of faith, of honor and of virtue, a duplication of your ancestors . . . [Pius XII, 1940, *Scritti e Discorsi*, II; *The Holy Father Speaks to Newlyweds*, pp. 6, 8].

Addressing the Italian Catholic Union of Midwives, Pius XII stated:

When a married couple esteem and appreciate the honor of bringing forth a new life whose advent they await with holy impatience, your role is an easy one. . . . Unfortunately, it is not always thus. Often the child is not wanted. Worse, it is feared. Under such conditions, how can people be ready to carry out their duty? In cases like this, your apostolate must be exercised in an effective and efficacious way; negatively, in the first place, by your refusal to co-operate in anything that is immoral; then constructively, by striving delicately to banish prejudices, apprehension or cowardly excuses in order to remove, as far as you are able, even external obstacles that may render the acceptance of motherhood a painful thing. . . .

*   *   *

There is no need for us to show you experienced women the great necessity today for this apostolate of esteem and love of the life of a new-born babe. Unfortunately, there are many cases where speaking, even cautiously, of children as a "blessing" is sufficient to provoke contradiction or even derision. Very often the idea and remarks about the great "burden" of children dominate. How opposed is such a frame of mind to God's plan and the language of Holy Scripture and even to sound reason and the sentiment of nature. If there are conditions and circumstances where, without violating God's law, parents can avoid the "blessing" of children, nevertheless these cases of "force majeure" do not authorize the perverting of ideas, the disparaging of values and the despising of the mother who has the courage and the honor to bring forth new life.

*   *   *

. . . It is you who, more by your whole manner of being and acting than by words, must help the young mother appreciate the greatness, the beauty, the nobility of that young life forming and living within her womb, born of her, carried in her arms and fed at her breast. . . .

. . . And the very labor which, after original sin, the mother must suffer to bring her child into the world is nothing but another bond drawing mother and child even closer. The more pain it has cost her, the more a mother loves her child. He Who moulds the mother's heart expresses this truth with profound and moving simplicity. "A woman about to give birth has sorrow because her hour has come. But when she has brought forth the child, she no longer remembers the anguish for her joy that a man is born into the world" (Jn. 16:21). And through the pen of St. Paul the Apostle, the Holy Ghost again shows the greatness and the joy of motherhood: God gives the child to the mother but in so doing He causes her to co-operate effectively in the unfolding of the flower whose seed He has placed within her. And this co-operation becomes a path leading to eternal salvation: "Woman will be saved by child-bearing" (1 Tim. 2:15).

*   *   *

Instill in the mind and heart of the mother and the father esteem, desire and joy for the new-born child; make them welcome it with love from the moment of its birth. The child formed in the womb of its mother is a gift of God (Ps. 126:3), Who entrusts it to the parents. How delicately, how charmingly, Holy Scripture describes the father sitting at table surrounded by his sons! They are the reward of the upright man, just as sterility is often the punishment of the sinner. Hear what Scripture says in the incomparable verses of the Psalm "Your wife (shall be) as a fruitful vine within your house, your children as olive shoots round about your table. Behold, thus is that man blessed who fears the Lord" (Ps. 127:3–4). But of the evildoer it is said: "May his posterity be given over to destruction; may their name be blotted out in the next generation" (Ps. 108:13).

At the birth of the child, hasten, like the Romans of old, to place it in the arms of the father but for an immeasurably more elevated reason. For the ancient Romans this meant a recognition of paternity and the authority deriving from it: but in your case, it is an act of homage to and recognition of the Creator, an invoking of the Divine blessing, the duty of carrying out the office given by God with devotion and affection. If the Lord praises and rewards the faithful servant for the fruitful use of his five talents (Mt. 25:21), what praise, what reward will He reserve for the father who has cherished and reared for Him the human life entrusted to him, a life worth more than all the gold and silver in the world! [Pius XII, 1951, *Apostolate of the Midwife; CM*, L, 52–55].

Pius XII, addressing the National Congress of the "Family Front" and the Association of Large Families, said:

Since, too, the primary office of matrimony is to be at the service of life, the expression of Our principal gratification and of Our paternal gratitude goes to those generous mothers and fathers who, for love of God and with trust in Him, courageously raise a large family [Pius XII, 1952, *Morality in Marriage; CM*, L, 311].

EDUCATION OF CHILDREN

Concerning the right and obligation of parents to educate their children, Leo XIII writes:

. . . Those who wish to tear society away from Christianity, go to the very roots and endeavour to corrupt the family. They do not allow themselves to be deterred from this attempt by the thought that this cannot be accomplished without inflicting upon parents the most cruel outrage; for to parents it belongs by virtue of natural right to educate their children to the ends which God has given them. It is a strict obligation laid upon parents to give all their care, and to neglect no effort to repulse energetically all unjust violence done to them in this matter, so that they may guard their exclusive authority in the education of their children . . . [Leo XIII, 1890, *Sapientiae Christianae; SW,* I, 162].

Benedict XV states that women should learn the necessity of religious education for their children, and that they should also demand it from civil authorities.

. . . Let Catholic women appeal to the duty that parents have of demanding religious instruction for their children; let them appeal to the obligation of the civil authority not to put any obstacles in their way; but above all let her show herself concerned of the necessity of seeking from the Church the most opportune rules of action and putting them at once into practice [Benedict XV, 1919, *Woman's Mission in Modern Society; CM,* XVII, 456].

PIUS XI asks, who has the right to educate? He answers his own question by stating:

In the first place comes the family, instituted directly by God for its peculiar purpose, the generation and formation of offspring. For this reason it has priority of nature and therefore of rights over civil society.

*   *   *

The Angelic Doctor with his wonted clearness of thought and

precision of style, says: "The father according to the flesh has in a particular way a share in that principle which in a manner universal is found in God. . . . The father is the principle of generation, of education and discipline and of everything that bears upon the perfecting of human life" (2–2, q. cii, a I).

The family therefore holds directly from the Creator the mission and hence the right to educate the offspring, a right inalienable because inseparably joined to a strict obligation, a right anterior to any right whatever of civil society and of the state, and therefore inviolable on the part of any power on earth.

That this right is inviolable St. Thomas proves as follows: "The child is naturally something of the father . . . so by natural right the child, before reaching the use of reason, is under the father's care. Hence it would be contrary to natural justice if the child, before the use of reason, were removed from the care of its parents, or if any disposition were made concerning him against the will of the parents" (2–2, q. x, a. 12). And as this duty on the part of the parents continues up to the time when the child is in a position to provide for himself, this same inviolable parental right of education also endures. "Nature intends not merely the generation of the offspring, but also its development and progress to the perfection of man considered as man, that is, to the state of virtue" says the same St. Thomas (3 — p., q. 41, a. I).

The wisdom of the Church in this matter is expressed with precision and clearness in the Codex of Canon Law: "Parents are under a grave obligation to see to the religious and moral education of their children, as well as to their physical and civic training, as far as they can, and moreover to provide for their temporal well-being" (c. 1113).

On this point the common sense of mankind is in such complete accord, that they would be in open contradiction with it who dared maintain that the children belong to the state before they belong to the family, and that the state has an absolute right over their education. Untenable is the reason they deduce, namely that man is born a citizen and hence belongs primarily to the state, not bearing in mind that before being a citizen man must exist; and existence does not come from the state, but from the parents, as Leo XIII wisely declared: "The children are something of the father, and as it were an extension of the person of the father. To be perfectly accurate, they enter into and become part of civil society, not directly by themselves, but through the family in which they were born. . . . And therefore the father's power is of such a nature that it cannot be destroyed or absorbed by the state; for it has the same origin as human life itself" (*Rerum Novarum*).

It does not follow from this that the parents' right to educate their children is absolute and despotic; for it is necessarily subordinated to the last end and to natural and divine law. On this point Leo XIII in another memorable Encyclical thus sums up the rights and duties of parents: "By nature parents have a right to the training of their children, but with this added duty that the education and instruction of the child be in accord with the end for which by God's blessing it was begotten. Therefore it is the duty of parents to make every effort to prevent any invasion of their rights in this matter, and to make absolutely sure that the education of their children remains under their own control, in keeping with their Christian duty, and above all to refuse to send them to those schools in which there is danger of imbibing the deadly poison of impiety" (*Sapientiae Christianae*).

*   *   *

It . . . belongs to the state to protect the rights of the child itself when the parents are found wanting either physically or morally in this respect, whether by default, incapacity, or misconduct, since, as has been shown, their right to educate is not an absolute and despotic one, but is dependent on the natural and divine law, and therefore subject alike to the authority and jurisdiction of the Church, and to the vigilance and administrative care of the state in view of the common good. Besides, the family is not a perfect society, that is, it has not in itself all the means necessary for its full development. In such cases, exceptional no doubt, the state does not put itself in the place of the family, but merely supplies deficiencies, and provides suitable means, always in conformity with the natural rights of the child and the supernatural rights of the Church [Pius XI, 1929, *Rappresentanti in Terra,* or *Divini Illius Magistri; SW,* II, 92, 97–99, 101].

Pius XII, speaking to newlyweds, said:
. . . According to the divine plan parents are the first educators of their own children. It is well nevertheless to recognize the fact that under actual conditions of life the necessary preoccupation of making a living makes the fulfillment of this essential duty difficult . . . [Pius XII, 1940, *Scritti e Discorsi,* II; *The Holy Father Speaks to Newlyweds,* p. 16].

And to the Eighth International Congress of Administrative Sciences, Pius XII said:
. . . Families have certain rights and liberties which the State must always protect; which it must never violate or sacrifice to a pretended common good. We have in mind, to cite a few examples, the right to honor and to a good reputation, the right and the freedom to worship the true God, the inherently primary right of parents over their children and their children's education [Pius XII, 1950, *The Modern State; CM,* XLIX, 461].

CO-OPERATION OF PARENTS WITH TEACHERS

Before a concourse of Women of Catholic Action, Pius XII remarked:
. . . However eminent school-teachers may be in their profession they will have little success in the formation of your children without your collaboration. . . . What a misfortune it would be if at home your indulgence and fond weakness were to undo all that has been done at school, at catechism or in Catholic associations, to form the character and foster the piety of your children! [Pius XII, 1941, *Women of Catholic Action; Clergy Review,* XXII, 137].

EDUCATORS MUST STRIVE TO UNDERSTAND YOUNG PEOPLE

Speaking to newlyweds, Pius XII said:

Instinct endows even irrational animals with affection for their young. Hence it should not be necessary to teach affection to newlyweds and future Christian parents. It could, none the less, come about that excessive severity or a lack of understanding would raise a sort of barrier between the hearts of the children and those of their parents. St. Paul said: "To the weak I became weak. . . . I became all things to all men, that I might save all" (1 Cor. 9:22). It is a great good quality to know how to become little with the little, children with the children, without compromising paternal or maternal authority in so doing . . . [Pius XII, 1940, *Scritti e Discorsi,* II; *The Holy Father Speaks to Newlyweds,* p. 39].

Pius XII said this to a Concourse of Women of Catholic Action:

Study the child in his tender age. If you know him well you will educate him well; you will not misconceive his character; you will come to understand him, knowing when to give way and when to be firm; a naturally good disposition does not fall to the lot of all the sons of men [Pius XII, 1941, Women of Catholic Action; *Clergy Review,* XXII, 135].

To the First International Congress of Teaching Sisters, Pope Pius XII said:

. . . It is not using empty words to say that young people have changed, have become quite different . . . the subject of frequent lament: young people are irreverent toward many things that formerly from childhood were naturally regarded with the greatest respect. . . .

It must be remembered also that this complaint about lack of understanding is not something new. It is one made in every generation and it is mutual between maturity and youth, parents and children, teachers and pupils. . . .

. . . try to reform young people and convince them by making them submit, to persuade them by force, would be useless and not always right. You will induce them very much better to give you their confidence if you, on your side strive to understand them and to make them understand themselves — save always in case of those immutable truths and values which admit of no change in the heart and mind of man.

Understanding young people does not mean approving and admitting everything they maintain in their ideas, their tastes, their whims, their false enthusiasm. It consists fundamentally in finding out what is solid in them and accepting this trustfully without remorse or anger; in discovering the origin of their deviations and errors which are often nothing but the unhappy attempt to solve real and difficult problems; and, finally, in following closely the vicissitudes and conditions of the present times.

* * *

. . . When you are with young people, it is not necessary to speak continually of God. But when you do so, you must speak in a way to command their attention: with genuine feeling arising from profound conviction. In this way, you will win the confidence of your pupils who will then allow themselves to be persuaded and guided by you [Pius XII, 1951, *On Educating Youth; CM, L, 377*].

PARENTS MUST PROVIDE RELIGIOUS TRAINING FOR CHILDREN

When writing to the archbishops and bishops of France, on education, Leo XIII stated:

. . . As regards family life, it is of the highest importance that the offspring of Christian marriages should be thoroughly instructed in the precepts of religion; and that the various studies by which youth is fitted for the world should be joined with that of religion. To divorce these is to wish that youth should be neutral as regards its duties to God; a system of education in itself fallacious, and particularly fatal in tender years, for it opens the door to atheism, and closes it on religion. Christian parents must therefore be careful that their children receive religious instruction as soon as they are capable of understanding it; and that nothing may, in the schools they attend, blemish their faith or their morals. Both the natural and the divine law impose this duty on them, nor can parents on any ground whatever be freed from this obligation . . . [Leo XIII, 1884, *Nobilissima Gallorum Gens; Tablet,* LXIII, 241].

Leo XIII speaks about the obligation of parents to educate their children, and then adds:
. . . They must, moreover, imbue these with the principles of Christian morality, and absolutely oppose their children frequenting schools where they are exposed to the fatal poison of impiety. When it is a question of the good education of youth, we have no right to fix a limit to the pains and labour that result, however great these may be. Those Catholics of all nationalities, who, at the expense of much money and more zeal, have erected schools for the education of their children, are worthy of being proposed for the admiration of all. It would be well if this beautiful example were followed wherever circumstances called for it . . . [Leo XIII, 1890, *Sapientiae Christianae; SW,* I, 162].

Concerning religious education Pius XI writes:
. . . The Church is indeed conscious of her divine mission to all mankind, and of the obligation which all men have to practise the one true religion; and therefore she never tires of defending her right, and of reminding parents of their duty, to have all Catholic-born children baptized and brought up as Christians. . . .

*   *   *

. . . Accordingly, unjust and unlawful is any monopoly, educational or scholastic, which, physically or morally, forces families to make use of government schools, contrary to the dictates of their Christian conscience, or contrary even to their legitimate preferences.

*   *   *

In fact it must never be forgotten that the subject of Christian education is man whole and entire, soul united to body in unity of nature, with all his faculties natural and supernatural, such as right reason and revelation show him to be. . . .

* * *

. . . Parents, therefore, and all who take their place in the work of education, should be careful to make right use of the authority given them by God, whose vicars in a true sense they are. This authority is not given for their own advantage, but for the proper upbringing of their children in a holy and filial "fear of God, the beginning of wisdom," on which foundation alone all respect for authority can rest securely; and without which, order, tranquillity, and prosperity, whether in the family or in society, will be imperiled [Pius XI, 1929, *Rappresentanti in Terra*, or *Divini Illius Magistri; SW*, II, 100, 102, 107, 112].

To Mexican Catholics, Pius XI wrote:

If Catholic Action cannot neglect the most humble and the most needy classes, of the laborers, of the peasants, of the emigrants, it has in other fields no less grave and inescapable duties. . . .

* * *

. . . We would have you provide that religious instruction should hold an intellectual primacy among students and educated Catholics.

* * *

The special conditions of your country oblige Us to recall the necessary, obligatory, inescapable care of the children, whose innocence is ensnared, whose education and Christian formation is thus so sorely tried. Two grave precepts are imposed on all Catholic Mexicans: the one negative, that is, to keep the children as far away as possible from the impious and corruptive school; the other positive, to give them complete and accurate religious instruction and the necessary assistance to maintain their spiritual life [Pius XI, 1937, *Firmissimam Constantiam; SW*, II, 382–383].

Pius XII, addressing the archbishops and bishops of the world concerning the formation of youth, stated:

. . . A formation which forgot or, worse still, deliberately neglected to direct the eyes and hearts of youth to the heavenly country would be an injustice to youth, an injustice against the inalienable duties and rights of the Christian family and an excess to which a check must be opposed, in the interests even of the people and of the State itself.

*   *   *

. . . The souls of children given to their parents by God and consecrated in Baptism with the royal character of Christ, are a sacred charge over which watched the jealous love of God. The same Christ Who pronounced the words "Suffer little children to come to me" has threatened, for all His mercy and goodness, with fearful evils, those who give scandal to those so dear to His Heart [Pius XII, 1939, *Summi Pontificatus; CM*, XXXVII, 905–906].

Exhorting newlyweds, Pius XII declared:

. . . By educating your children to a life that is deeply and courageously Christian, you will give them and yourself the best guarantee of a happy life in this world and of a happy reunion in the next [Pius XII, 1940, *Scritti e Discorsi*, II; *The Holy Father Speaks to Newlyweds*, p. 6].

In an address to the Inter-American Congress on Catholic Education, Pius XII said:

See that your children as they advance in age receive religious instruction . . . not forgetting that both the full and profound consciousness of religious truths, as well as doubts and difficulties, usually manifest themselves in the last years of higher studies. . . . For this reason, religious instruction demands with every right a place of honor in the programs of universities and centers of advanced studies. . . .

*   *   *

. . . Counteract the lack of principles of the world today, which measures everything by the criterion of success, with an education which makes a youth capable of discerning between truth and error, good and evil, right and injustice, planting firmly in his soul the pure sentiments of love, fraternity and fidelity [Pius XII, 1948, *Education and the Modern Environment; CM,* XLVII, 119].

To the Italian Women of Catholic Action, Pius XII said:
. . . Keep before the eyes of the child, from its early years, the commandments of God and accustom it to observe them. The youth of today no less than that of former days is prepared and is ready to do good and to serve God, but it must be educated to do so.

* * *

Educate youth to obedience and respect for authority. This is simple when man is submissive to God and recognizes the absolute value of His commandments. For the unbeliever and the man who denies God, there cannot be any true, just and ordered authority because "there exists no authority except from God" (Rom. 13, 1). Man can neither rule nor be ruled by fear and force [Pius XII, 1949, *Woman's Apostolate; CM,* XLVII, 689].

In an address proclaiming St. John de La Salle the Patron Saint of All Teachers and Student Teachers, Pius XII remarked:
The saying of St. Bonaventure that "the only true educator is one who can kindle in the heart of his pupil the vision of beauty, illumine it with the light of truth and infuse virtue" is particularly appropriate at the present time when the education of the young is not only frequently at variance with the principles of true moral training but is often Godless and irreligious and harmful in the extreme. For this reason Holy Mother Church cherishes with a solicitous affection those whose duty it is to educate children, all the more so as the welfare and development of the Christian Community depend on them in no small measure [Pius XII, 1950, *Duty of Educators; CM,* XLVIII, 511].

To the Association of Large Families, Pius XII declared:
. . . To strive on behalf of the school and religious education:

this, too, is a precious contribution to the welfare of the family, as also are fostering therein of a healthy naturalness and simplicity of habits, the strengthening of religious convictions, the development around it of an atmosphere of Christian purity which will free it from deleterious outside influences and from all those morbid excitations which give rise to disordinate passions in the minds of youths [Pius XII, 1951, *Morality in Marriage; CM*, L, 307].

In a radio address to a national convention of Austrian Catholics in Vienna, Pius XII said:

. . . In guarding your faith you must insist that the Catholic school be assured and preserved for your children. For what good is Catholic education at home if the schools undo what the home has carefully built up. . . .

*　　*　　*

. . . Sacred to you parents must be the Christian upbringing of your children. Sacred to you children must be the Fourth Commandment — respectful obedience to your parents [Pius XII, 1952, *To Austrian Catholics;* CM, LI, 49–50].

Addressing the pupils of Don Bosco School, in London, England, Pius XII stated:

Now a word of advice to you, parents and relatives of these children. We are well aware of the difficulties and worries you often meet with, which prevent you from doing as much as you would like for your children. But try, at least, to help the priest in his educational work as much as you can. Sad to say, it has sometimes happened that some families have only succeeded in destroying all that has been built up in the souls of their children in the beautiful atmosphere of the chapel or the classroom . . . [Pius XII, 1953, *Allocution to the Pupils of the Don Bosco School; Catholic Documents*, XIII, 5].

VOCATION

About the right to choose one's state of life, Leo XIII writes:

In choosing a state of life, it is indisputable that all are at full liberty either to follow the counsel of Jesus Christ as to virginity, or to enter into the bonds of marriage . . . [Leo XIII, 1891, *Rerum Novarum; SW*, I, 173].

Concerning the vocation to the priesthood, Pius XI states:
. . . The first and most natural place where the flowers of the sanctuary should almost spontaneously grow and bloom, remains always the truly and deeply Christian family. Most of the saintly bishops and priests whose praise the Church declares, owe the beginning of their vocation and their holiness to the example and teaching of a father strong in faith and manly virtues, of a pure and devoted mother, and of a family in which the love of God and neighbor, joined with simplicity of life, has reigned supreme.

*   *   *

. . . Blessed are those Christian parents who are able to accept without fear the vocations of their sons, and see in them a signal honor of their family and a mark of the special love and providence of our Lord. Still more blessed, if, as was often the case in ages of greater faith, they make such divine visitations the object of their earnest prayer.

Yet it must be confessed with sadness that only too often parents seem to be unable to resign themselves to the priestly or religious vocations of their children. Such parents have no scruple in opposing the divine call with objections of all kinds. They even have recourse to means which can imperil not only the vocation to a more perfect state, but also the very conscience and the eternal salvation of those souls they ought to hold so dear. This happens all too often in the case even of parents who glory in being sincerely Christian and Catholic, especially in the higher and more cultured classes. . . . It hardly does honor to those higher classes of society, which are on the whole so scantily represented in the ranks of the clergy. The lack of vocations in families of the middle and upper classes may be partly explained by the dissipations of modern life, the seductions, which especially in the larger cities, prematurely awaken the passions of youth; the schools in many places which scarcely conduce to the development of vocations. Nevertheless, it must be admitted that such a scarcity reveals a deplorable falling off of faith in the families themselves . . . [Pius XI, 1935, *Ad Catholici Sacerdotii; SW*, II, 427–429].

In regard to voluntary celibacy according to the evangelical counsels, Pius XII writes:

But let us remember that for nigh on to 20 centuries, in every generation, thousands and thousands of men and women, from among the best, in order to follow the counsels of Christ, freely renounced the possibility of a family of their own and the sacred duties and rights of married life.

*   *   *

. . . But, if they abandon the ordinary way and leave the beaten track, they do not desert it, but rather consecrate themselves to the service of mankind with a complete disregard for themselves and their own interests by an act incomparably broader in its scope, more all-embracing and universal.

*   *   *

When one thinks of young girls and women who willingly renounce Matrimony in order to consecrate themselves to a higher life of contemplation, sacrifice and charity, there comes at once to the lips the word that explains it: vocation. It is the only word that can describe so lofty a sentiment [Pius XII, 1945, *Woman's Duties in Social and Political Life; CM*, XLIII, 707–708].

To the Italian Women of Catholic Action, Pius XII said:

Do not forget however that among woman's vocations there is also the religious vocation, the state of a virgin consecrated to God. This observation is all the more opportune today, because with the deserved esteem for apostolic labor in the world, there might center, almost imperceptibly, a shadow of naturalism, which would cloud the beauty and the fertile value that is to be found in the complete gift of the heart and life to God.

The apostolate of the Church today can hardly be conceived without the collaboration of nuns in works of charity, in the schools, in the assistance of the priestly ministry and in the missions. It is, therefore, up to Italian women to assure for Italy the necessary vocations. Work to encourage them, and you know that the beneficial results of virgins consecrated to God are to be seen returning to the families themselves in various forms [Pius XII, 1949, *Woman's Apostolate; CM*, XLVII, 687].

Speaking About Religious Life to the First International Congress of Teaching Sisters, Pius XII said:
Chastity and virginity (which imply also the inner renunciation of all sensual affection) do not estrange souls from this world. They rather awaken and develop the energies needed for wider and higher offices beyond the limits of individual families. Today there are many teaching and nursing Sisters who, in the best sense of the word, are nearer to life than the average person in the world [Pius XII, 1951, *On Educating Youth; CM*, L, 378].

Pius XII states that procreation does not belong to the essence of a complete human being.
. . . This is a high and noble office, but it is one that does not belong to the essence of a complete human being as though in the case when the natural generative tendency is not brought into play there would be some diminution of the human person. Renunciation of this act — especially if done for the noblest of motives — is not a mutilation of personal and spiritual values. Of this renunciation for the love of the Kingdom of God Our Lord has said: "Not all can accept this teaching; but those to whom it has been given" (Mt. 19:11) [Pius XII, 1951, *Apostolate of the Midwife; CM*, L, 61].

MIND AND CHARACTER TRAINING

Concerning character training, Pius XI writes:
. . . The inclinations of the will, if they are bad, must be repressed from childhood, but such as are good must be fostered, and the mind, particularly of children, should be strengthened with the aids of divine grace, in the absence of which no one can curb

evil desires, nor can his discipline and formation be brought to complete perfection by the Church. For Christ has provided her with heavenly doctrine and divine sacraments, that He might make her an effectual teacher of men [Pius XI, 1930, CC; *SW*, II, 167].

Speaking before a concourse of Women of Catholic Action, Pius XII stressed the training of the mind and of the character:

Train the mind of your children. Do not give them wrong ideas or wrong reasons for things; whatever their questions may be, do not answer them with evasions or untrue statements which their minds rarely accept; but take occasion from them lovingly and patiently to train their minds, which want only to open to the truth and to grasp it with the first ingenuous gropings of their reasoning and reflective powers. Who can say what many a genius may not owe to the prolonged and trustful questions of childhood at the home fireside!

Train the character of your children. Correct their faults, encourage and cultivate their good qualities and co-ordinate them with that stability which will make for resolution in after life. Your children, conscious as they grow up and as they begin to think and will, that they are guided by a good paternal will constant and strong, free from violence and anger, not subject to weakness or inconsistency, will learn in time to see therein the interpreter of another and higher will, the will of God, and so they will plant in their souls the seeds of those moral habits which fashion and sustain a character, train it to self-control in moments of crisis and to courage in the face of conflict or sacrifice, and imbue it with a deep sense of Christian duty [Pius XII, 1941, *Women of Catholic Action; Clergy Review,* XXII, 135].

And Pius XII writes:

Immoderate pursuit of pleasure and lack of moral discipline likewise seek to invade even the ranks of Catholic youth. . . . Counteract this with the education of self-control, of sacrifice and of renunciation, beginning with smaller things and gradually going on to greater ones. . . . Promote education of fidelity in fulfillment of one's own duties, of sincerity, serenity and purity, especially in the years of development into maturity. . . . Try to arouse and to mold a sense of responsibility and to remind them that liberty is not the only one among all the human values, although it is numbered among the foremost, but that it has its limits, intrinsic in the unescapable norms of decency and extrinsic in the correlative rights of others, both as regards the rights of each one in particular as well as the rights of society in general . . . [Pius XII, 1948, *Education and the Modern Environment; CM,* XLVII, 120].

Pius XII instructed the Italian Women of Catholic Action as follows:

Counteract the desire for luxury and pleasure with an education in frankness and simplicity! Youth must learn again to control itself and face privations. It must not happen that youth should burden parents with requests that parents cannot satisfy. Simplicity of life and economy have at all times been characteristic of the Italian people. They must remain so, because even the national economy requires them [Pius XII, 1949, *Woman's Apostolate; CM,* XLVII, 689].

PATRIOTISM

Speaking about loyalty to one's country, Pius XI said to German youths:

No one would think of preventing German youths from building a true ethnical community in a noble love of freedom and loyalty to their country. What We object to is the voluntary and systematic antagonism raised between national education and religious duty. That is why We tell the young: Sing your hymns to freedom, but do not forget the freedom of the children of God. Do not drag the nobility of that freedom in the mud of sin and sensuality. He who sings hymns of loyalty to his terrestrial country should not, for that reason, become unfaithful to God and His Church, or a deserter and traitor to His heavenly country . . . [Pius XI, 1937, *Mit brennender Sorge; SW,* II, 334].

About the formation of youth, Pius XII remarked:

Undoubtedly, that formation should aim as well at the preparation of youth to fulfill with intelligent understanding and pride those offices of a noble patriotism which give to one's earthly fatherland all due measure of love, self-devotion and service . . . [Pius XII, 1939, *Summi Pontificatus; CM*, XXXVII, 905].

SEX EDUCATION

In his encyclical Christian Education of Youth, *Pius XI writes:*

Another grave danger is that naturalism which nowadays invades the field of education in that most delicate matter of purity of morals. Far too common is the error of those who with dangerous assurance and under an ugly term propagate a so-called sex education, falsely imagining they can forearm youth against the dangers of sensuality by means purely natural, such as a foolhardy initiation and precautionary instruction for all indiscriminately, even in public; and, worse still, by exposing them at an early age to the occasions, in order to accustom them, it is argued, and to harden them, as it were, against such dangers.

Such persons grievously err in refusing to recognize the inborn weakness of human nature, and that law of which the Apostle speaks, "as warring against the law of my mind" (Rom. 7:23), and also in ignoring the experience of facts, from which it is clear that, particularly in young people, evil practices are the effect not so much of ignorance of intellect as of weakness of a will exposed to dangerous occasions, and unsupported by the means of grace.

*   *   *

Such is our misery and inclination to sin, that often in the very things considered to be remedies against sin, we find occasions for and inducements to sin itself. Hence it is of the highest importance that a good father, while discussing with his son a matter so delicate, should be well on his guard and not descend to details, nor refer to the various ways in which this infernal hydra destroys with its poison so large a portion of the world.

Otherwise it may happen that instead of extinguishing this fire, he unwittingly stirs or kindles it in the simple and tender heart of the child. Speaking generally, during the period of childhood it suffices to employ those remedies which produce the double effect of opening the door to the virtue of purity and closing the door upon vice.

False also and harmful to Christian education is the so-called method of "coeducation." This, too, by many of its supporters, is founded upon naturalism and the denial of original sin; but by all, upon a deplorable confusion of ideas that mistakes a leveling promiscuity and equality, for the legitimate association of the sexes. The Creator has ordained and disposed perfect union of sexes only in matrimony, and, with varying degrees of contact, in the family and in society. Besides there is not in nature itself, which fashions the two quite different in organism, in temperament, in abilities, anything to suggest that there can be or ought to be promiscuity, and much less equality, in the training of the two sexes. These in keeping with the wonderful designs of the Creator are destined to complement each other in the family and in society, precisely because of their differences, which therefore ought to be maintained and encouraged during their years of formation, with the necessary distinction and corresponding separation, according to age and circumstances. These principles, with due regard to time and place, must in accordance with Christian prudence, be applied to all schools, particularly in the most delicate and decisive period of formation, that, namely, of adolescence. So, too, in gymnastic exercises and deportment, special care must be had of Christian modesty in young women and girls, which is so gravely impaired by any kind of exhibition in public [Pius XI, 1929, *Rappresentanti in Terra*, or *Divini Illius Magistri; SW*, II, 108–110].

To a concourse of Women of Catholic Action, Pius XII said:
. . . With the discretion of a mother and a teacher, and thanks to the open-hearted confidences with which you have been able to inspire your children, you will not fail to watch for and to

discern the moment in which certain unspoken questions have occurred to their minds and are troubling their senses. It will then be your duty to your daughters, the father's duty to your sons, carefully and delicately to unveil the truth as far as it appears necessary, to give a prudent, true and Christian answer to those questions, and set their minds at rest. If imparted by the lips of Christian parents, at the proper time, in the proper measure and with the proper precautions, the revelation of the mysterious and marvelous laws of life will be received by them with reverence and gratitude, and will enlighten their minds with far less danger than if they learned them haphazardly . . . [Pius XII, 1941, *Women of Catholic Action; Clergy Review,* XXII, 136].

To the Italian Women of Catholic Action, Pius XII declared:
Educate youth in purity. Help youth when an explaining word of advice and guidance is necessary. Do not forget that a good education must embrace the whole life, and in this sphere especially the habit of self-control is the best formation [Pius XII, 1949, *Women's Apostolate; CM,* XLVII, 689].

To the Italian Catholic Union of Midwives, Pius XII said:
. . . Banish from your minds the cult of pleasure and do your best to stop the diffusion of literature that thinks it a duty to describe in full detail the intimacy of conjugal life under the pretense of instructing, directing, and reassuring. To calm the timid consciences of couples, common sense, natural instinct, and a brief instruction on the clear and simple maxims of Christian morality are usually sufficient. If under special circumstances a girl who is engaged or a young wife needs further explanations on some particular point, you must instruct her with delicacy and in conformity with the natural law and the healthy conscience of a Christian [Pius XII, 1951, *Apostolate of the Midwife; CM,* L, 63].

Speaking to the Fifth International Congress of Psychotherapy and Clinical Psychology, Pius XII stated:
A word also on the method sometimes employed by the psy-

chologist to liberate the ego of its inhibition in the case of aberration in the sexual domain. We refer to complete sexual initiation, which would not pass over anything in silence, leave nothing in obscurity. Is there not therein a harmful overestimation of knowledge in these matters?

There is also an efficacious sexual education which, in entire safety, teaches with calmness and objectivity what the young man should know for his own personal conduct and his relationship with those with whom he is brought into contact. For the rest, the accent will be placed principally, in sexual education — as moreover, in all education — upon self-mastery and religious training. The Holy See published certain norms in this connection shortly after the Encyclical of Pius XI *On Christian Marriage* (Holy Office, March 21, 1931 — *Acta Apostolicae Sedis,* Vol. 23, 1931, p. 118). These norms have not been rescinded, neither expressly nor via facti (by way of fact) [Pius XII, 1953, *On Psychotherapy and Religion; CM,* LI, 431].

CARE OF CHILDREN

Leo XIII writes:

As regards children, they ought to submit to the parents and obey them, and give them honour for conscience' sake; while on the other hand, parents are bound to give all care and watchful thought to the education of their offspring and their virtuous bringing up: "Father . . . bring them up [that is, your children] in the discipline and correction of the Lord" (Eph. 6:4). From this we see clearly that the duties of husbands and wives are neither few nor light; although to married people who are good, these burdens become not only bearable but agreeable, owing to the strength which they gain through the sacrament [Leo XIII, 1880, *Arcanum; SW,* I, 30–31].

Pius XI has this to say:

Let, then, those who are about to enter on married life, approach that state well disposed and well prepared. . . . It will also help them, if they behave toward their cherished offspring as

God wills: that is, that the father be truly a father, and the mother truly a mother. Through their devout love and unwearying care, the home, though it suffer the want and hardship of this valley of tears, may become for the children in its own way a foretaste of that paradise of delight in which the Creator placed the first man of the human race. Thus will they be able to bring up their children as perfect men and perfect Christians; they will instill into them a sound understanding of the Catholic Church, and will give them such a disposition and love for their fatherland as duty and gratitude demand [Pius XI, 1930, CC; *SW*, II, 167].

To newlyweds, Pius XII said:

You, too, my dear newlyweds, have made, make and will make cherished plans for the future of your children. Unhappy the parents who would not make them! But be careful that your plans be not entirely earthly and human . . . [Pius XII, 1940, *Scritti e Discorsi*, II; *The Holy Father Speaks to Newlyweds*, p. 6].

Speaking about aid to youth, Pius XII said:

Let us use all the means that modern progress offers or recommends to provide an effective remedy for present ills. . . . For, as all know, there would not be such a mass of delinquents in the common jails if greater and more suitable means were taken to prevent especially juvenile delinquency . . . [Pius XII, 1946, *Aid to Youth in the World Crisis; CM*, XLIV, 132].

To the Italian Catholic Union of Midwives, Pius XII said:

. . . In the case of a grown-up person, an act of love may suffice for obtaining sanctifying grace and making up for the lack of Baptism. To the child still unborn or the child just born this path is not open. . . . It is easy to understand the great importance of seeing that Baptism is given to a child deprived completely of the use of reason, in grave danger or certain of dying.

There is no doubt that this duty binds the parents in the first place . . .[Pius XII, 1951, *Apostolate of the Midwife; CM,* L, 53–54].

MUTUAL AID AND COMPANIONSHIP

Leo XIII writes:

. . . The mutual duties of husband and wife have been defined and their several rights accurately established. They are bound, namely, to have such feelings for one another as to cherish always very great mutual love, to be ever faithful to their marriage vow, and to give to one another an unfailing and unselfish help . . . [Leo XIII, 1880, *Arcanum; SW,* I, 30].

Concerning the love and companionship that should exist between husband and wife, Pius XI writes:

These parties, let it be noted, not fettered but adorned by the golden bond of the sacrament, not hampered but assisted, should strive with all their might to the end that their wedlock, not only through the power and symbolism of the sacrament, but also through their spirit and manner of life, may be and remain always the living image of that most fruitful union of Christ with the Church, which is to be venerated as the sacred token of most perfect love.

*   *   *

No one can fail to admire the divine Wisdom, Holiness, and Goodness which, while respecting the dignity and happiness of husband and wife, has provided so bountifully for the conservation and propagation of the human race by a single, chaste, and sacred fellowship of nuptial union [Pius XI, 1930, CC; *SW,* II, 140].

To the Italian Catholic Union of Midwives, Pius XII said:

The "values of the human person" and the need of respecting them is a subject which has occupied writers more and more for twenty years. In many of their writings even the specifically sexual act has its place assigned to it in the service of the married couple. The proper and more profound meaning of the conjugal right must consist in this that the union of the bodies is the expression and the physical manifestation of personal and mutual affection [Pius XII, 1951, *Apostolate of the Midwife; CM*, L, 59].

HAPPINESS IN MARRIAGE

Leo XIII writes:

To sum up all in a few words: there would be a calm and quiet constancy in marriage if married people would gather strength and life from the virtue of religion alone, which imparts to us resolution and fortitude. For religion would enable them to bear tranquilly and even gladly the trials of their state; such as, for instance, the faults that they discover in one another, the difference of temper and character, the weight of a mother's cares, the wearing anxiety about the education of children, reverses of fortune, and the sorrows of life [Leo XIII, 1880, *Arcanum; SW*, I, 45].

Pius XI states that happiness in marriage consists in obedience to God's law and in co-operation with His divine grace.

. . . In fine, in spite of what others may wish to assert and spread abroad by word of mouth or in writing, let husband and wife resolve: to stand fast to the commandments of God in all things that matrimony demands; always to render to each other the assistance of mutual love; to preserve the honor of chastity; not to lay profane hands on the stable nature of the bond; to use the rights given them by marriage in a way that will be always Christian and sacred, more especially in the first years of wedlock, so that should there be need of continency afterward, custom will have made it easier for each to preserve it.

In order that they may make this firm resolution, keep it and put it into practice, an oft-repeated consideration of their state of life, and a diligent reflection on the sacrament they have received, will be of great assistance to them. Let them constantly keep in mind, that they have been sanctified and strengthened for the duties and for the dignity of their state by a special sacrament, the efficacious power of which, although it does not impress a character, is undying. . . .

*   *   *

Yet in order that the grace of this sacrament may produce its full fruit, there is need, as we have already pointed out, of the co-operation of the parties; which consists in their striving to fulfill their duties to the best of their ability and with unwearied effort. For just as in the natural order men must apply the powers given them by God with their own toil and diligence that these may exercise their full vigor, failing which, no profit is gained, so also men must diligently and unceasingly use the powers given them by the grace which is laid up in the soul by this sacrament. Let not, then, those who are joined in matrimony neglect the grace of the sacrament which is in them; for, in applying themselves to the careful observance, however laborious, of their duties they will find the power of that grace becoming more and more effectual as time goes on . . . [Pius XI, 1930, CC; *SW*, II, 165–166].

Pius XII writes:

. . . Not only the common work of external life but also intellectual and spiritual endowment, even the depths of spirituality in conjugal love as such, have been put by the will of nature and the Creator at the service of our descendants. By its nature, perfect married life means also the complete dedication of the parents for the benefit of their children, and in its strength and tenderness, conjugal love is itself a postulate of the most sincere care for the offspring and the guarantee of its being carried out (St. Thomas 3 p. q. 29 a. 2 in c. Supplmt. q. 49 a. 2 ad I).

*   *   *

Some people are of the opinion that happiness in marriage is in direct proportion to mutual enjoyment in conjugal relations. This is not so. Happiness in marriage is in direct proportion to the respect the couple have for each other even in their intimate relations: not that they should deem immoral and refuse that which nature offers and the Creator has given, but because the respect and the mutual esteem it generates is one of the strongest elements of a pure, hence, more tender love.

In the performance of your duties, oppose, as much as you can, the impetus of this refined hedonism which is empty of all spiritual worth and unworthy of Christian couples. Show how nature has given the instinctive desire for enjoyment and approves of it in lawful wedlock but not as an end in itself; that it is something that serves life . . . [Pius XII, 1951, *Apostolate of the Midwife; CM, L,* 60–61, 63].

To the National Congress of the "Family Front" and the Association of Large Families, Pius XII said:

. . . To overcome the multiple trials of conjugal life, what is of the greatest worth is a living faith and a frequent reception of the Sacraments, whence pour forth torrents of strength of whose efficacy those living outside the Church cannot easily form a clear idea. . . . It may be, beloved sons and daughters, that one day it will fall to you to find your courage wavering under the violence of the tempest which doctrines, subversive of a healthy and normal conception of Christian marriage, unleash around you and even more dangerously into the bosom of the family. Have confidence! The energies of nature and especially the strength of grace with which Our Lord has enriched your souls in the Sacrament of Matrimony are as a firm rock, against which the waves of a storm-tossed sea break powerlessly . . . [Pius XII, 1951, *Morality in Marriage; CM, L,* 311].

BLESSINGS OF A HAPPY MARRIAGE

Leo XIII writes:

If, then, we consider the end of the divine institution of marriage, we shall see very clearly that God intended it to be a most fruitful source of individual benefit and of public welfare. Not only, in strict truth, was marriage instituted for the propagation of the human race, but also that the lives of husbands and wives might be made better and happier. This comes about in many ways: by their lightening each other's burdens through mutual help; by constant and faithful love; by having all their possessions in common; and by the heavenly grace which flows from the sacrament. Marriage also can do much for the good of families: for, so long as it is conformable to nature and in accordance with the counsels of God, it has power to strengthen union of heart in the parents; to secure the holy education of children; to attemper the authority of the father by the example of the divine authority; to render children obedient to their parents, and servants obedient to their masters. From such marriages as these the State may rightly expect a race of citizens animated by a good spirit and filled with reverence and love for God, recognizing it as their duty to obey those who rule justly and lawfully, to love all, and to injure no one [Leo XIII, 1880, *Arcanum; SW,* I, 37].

Pius XI calls children the first blessing of marriage and refers to them as "citizens with the Saints and members of God's household," in the words of St. Paul (Eph. 2:19); then he continues:
For although Christian spouses, even if sanctified themselves, cannot transmit sanctification to their progeny, nay, although the very natural process of generating life has become the way of death by which original sin is passed on to posterity, nevertheless, they share to some extent in the blessings of that primeval marriage of Paradise, since it is theirs to offer their offspring to the Church in order that by this most fruitful Mother of the children of God they may be regenerated through the laver of Baptism unto supernatural justice and finally be made living members of Christ, partakers of immortal life, and heirs of that eternal glory to which we all aspire from our inmost heart [Pius XI, 1930, CC; *SW,* II, 130].

Speaking to the Catholic women of Rome on the duties of woman in social and political life, Pius XII remarked:
The result of a genuine marriage union involves more than children when God grants them to the married couple, and the material and spiritual advantages that accrue to mankind from family life. The whole civilized world, all its branches, peoples,

even the Church itself — in a word, everything really good in mankind — benefits by the happy results when this family life is orderly and flourishing and when the young are accustomed to look up to it, honor it and love it as a holy ideal [Pius XII, 1945, *Woman's Duties in Social and Political Life; CM,* XLIII, 707].

EVIL OF UNHALLOWED MARRIAGE

Leo XIII writes:

Would that the teaching of those who reject what is super-natural, besides being full of falsehood and injustice, were not also the fertile source of much detriment and calamity! But it is easy to see at a glance the greatness of the evil which unhallowed marriages have brought, and ever will bring, on the whole of human society.

From the beginning of the world, indeed, it was divinely ordained that things instituted by God and by nature should be proved by us to be the more profitable and salutary the more they remain unchanged in their full integrity. For God, the Maker of all things, well knowing what was good for the nature and preservation of each of His creatures, so ordered them by His will and mind that each might adequately attain the end for which it was made. If the rashness or wickedness of human agency venture to change or disturb that order of things which has been constituted with fullest foresight, then the designs of infinite wisdom and usefulness begin either to be hurtful or cease to be profitable, partly because through the change undergone they have lost their power of benefiting, and partly because God chooses to inflict punishment on the pride and audacity of man. Now, those who deny that marriage is holy, and who relegate it, stripped of all sacredness, to the class of common things, uproot thereby the foundations of nature. They not only resist the designs of Providence, but, so far as they can, they destroy the order that God has ordained. No one, therefore, should wonder if from such insane and impious attempts there spring up a crop of evils pernicious in the highest degree both to the salvation of souls and to the safety of the commonwealth [Leo XIII, 1880, *Arcanum; SW,* I, 36–37].

Speaking about perverted individualism in the married state, Pius XII says:

But where the two sexes, forgetful of that intimate harmony willed and established by God, give themselves up to perverted individualism, where these mutual relations are governed by selfishness and covetousness, when they do not collaborate by mutual accord for the service of mankind and according to the designs of God and nature, when the young, scouting their responsibilities, silly and frivolous in spirit and conduct, render themselves unfit physically and morally for the holy state of Matrimony: then the common good of human society, in the temporal as well as the spiritual order, is gravely compromised and the Church of God herself trembles, not for her existence — for she has divine promises — but for the larger achievements of her mission to men [Pius XII, 1945, *Woman's Duties in Social and Political Life; CM,* XLIII, 707].

Chapter III

THE FAMILY

In Catholic doctrine the family is the primary and essential cell of society, anterior to every other kind of society, and having rights and duties which rest immediately upon nature.

God has appointed the parents as the natural providers for the material and spiritual good of their offspring. And, since the influence of the home upon the child is so great, the family should be governed by the rules of Christian life, so that each member will develop the virtues proper to members of Church and civil society; the family is the cradle of all social life.

The father of a family has the right and the responsibility of providing for his family. Hence such social and economic methods should be adopted that the head of the family can support himself, his wife, and his children according to his station in life.

Woman is by nature meant to be a mother. Since motherhood naturally demands that the average mother spend most of her time in caring for her home and her children, it is a serious evil when mothers of families are literally forced to engage in gainful occupation outside of the home.

However, woman's participation in public life is necessary at the present time in order that she might help man to counteract the bad influences which seek to ruin the home and the family. Furthermore, woman's dignity demands that she collaborate with man toward the total good of society.

Both the traditional fundamental truths and applications to modern conditions characterize the pronouncements of the popes on family life, but especially is there exhortation to defend family values against attack by exaggerated statism and a false concept of the nature of man.

FAMILY AND THE STATE

Speaking about the chief duties of Christian citizens, Leo XIII states:

. . . The family is the cradle of civil society, and it is for the most part in the surroundings of the home that the destiny of states is prepared . . . [Leo XIII, 1890, *Sapientiae Christianae; SW*, I, 162].

About family rights Leo XIII writes:

. . . Thus we have the family — the "society" of a man's own household; a society limited indeed in number, but a true "society," anterior to every kind of State or nation, with rights and duties of its own, totally independent of the commonwealth. . . .

. . . Since the domestic household is anterior both in idea and in fact to the gathering of men into a commonwealth, the former must necessarily have rights and duties which are prior to those of the latter, and which rest more immediately on nature. If the citizens of a State, if the families, on entering into association and fellowship, experienced at the hands of the State hindrance instead of being protected, such association were rather to be repudiated than sought after [Leo XIII, 1891, *Rerum Novarum; SW*, I, 173–174].

Concerning marriage and the family, Pius XI states:

Just as matrimony and the right of its natural use are of divine origin, so likewise are the constitution and fundamental prerogative of the family fixed and determined by the Creator . . . [Pius XI, 1937, *Divini Redemptoris; SW*, II, 352].

Speaking of the rights of the family, Pius XII states:

. . . There would be danger lest the primary and essential cell of society, the family, with its well-being and its growth, should come to be considered from the narrow standpoint of national power, and lest it be forgotten that man and the family are by nature anterior to the State, and that the Creator has given to both of them powers and rights and has assigned them a mission and a charge that correspond to undeniable natural requirements [Pius XII, 1939, *Summi Pontificatus; CM,* XXXVII, 904].

To newlyweds the Holy Father declared:
The family is the foundation of society. Just as the human body is made up of living cells which are not merely placed in juxtaposition, but which constitute an organic whole by their intimate and constant relationships, so also society is formed, not of a conglomeration of individuals, scattered beings, appearing one instant only to vanish the next, but rather of the economic community and moral solidarity of the families, which, handing down from generation to generation the precious heritage of the common ideal, of a common civilization, of a common religious faith, assure the cohesion and continuity of social bonds. St. Augustine noted this fifteen centuries ago when he wrote that the family should be the first element and, as it were, a little cell of the city . . . (*De civitate Dei,* 1, 19, ch. 16) . . . [Pius XII, 1940, *Scritti e Discorsi,* II; *The Holy Father Speaks to Newlyweds,* pp. 32–33].

About the family and the State, Pius XII writes:
On such a base especially rest the two main pillars, the fabric of human society as conceived and willed by God; the family and the State. Resting on such a foundation they can fulfill securely and perfectly their respective roles: the family as the source and school of life, the State as guardian of the law, which, like society in general itself, has its proximate origin and its end in the complete man, in the human person, the image of God [Pius XII, 1946, *The Church — Foundation of Society; CM,* XLIV, 200].

To the pupils and teachers for adult education, Pius XII remarked:
. . . But is it not perhaps too often forgotten that the basis of society, the very center of education and of every culture, is the family? . . . Could one believe that it is not necessary to

learn the supreme art of governing the family unit, wherein man uses, as far as possible, all his faculties of mind and heart, all his qualities and resources? . . .

*   *   *

Although the family is the foundation of all human culture, it must be developed within the cultural unit of society. By that is meant the sum of relations, both social and juridical, that unite man to his fellowmen and to civil authority . . . [Pius XII, 1953, *Discourse to the Pupils and Teachers for Adult Education; Catholic Documents,* No. 11, pp. 25–26].

HOME INFLUENCE

About family decay Leo XIII writes:

. . . For as an unsound tree produces decayed branches and miserable fruit, so the sad blot which depraves families is contagious, and becomes a cause of vice and sin in each individual member. On the contrary, if the family is governed by the rules of Christian life, each member of it will gradually become accustomed to cherish religion and piety, to reject with horror all false and pernicious doctrines, to practise virtue, to render obedience to the authorities, and to repress the insatiable egotism which so greatly debases and enfeebles human nature . . . [Leo XIII, 1878, *Inscrutabili; SW,* I, 10–11].

Again, he writes:

. . . Always and everywhere account must be taken of the great influence exercised over the souls of children by home education. If the young find in the home the rule of a virtuous life, and, as it were, a practical school of Christian virtue, the salvation of society in the future is in great part guaranteed [Leo XIII, 1890, *Sapientiae Christianae; SW,* I, 162–163].

Concerning the influence of the Christian home Pius XI writes:

The first natural and necessary element in this environment, as regards education, is the family, and this precisely because so ordained by the Creator Himself. Accordingly, that education, as a rule, will be more effective and lasting which is received in a well-ordered and well-disciplined Christian family. And it will be all the more efficacious in proportion to the clear and constant good example set, first by the parents, and then by the other members of the household.

*   *   *

. . . We wish to call your attention in a special manner to the present-day lamentable decline in family education. The offices and professions of a transitory and earthly life, which are certainly of far less importance, are prepared for by long and careful study; whereas for the fundamental duty and obligation of educating their children, many parents have little or no preparation, immersed as they are in temporal cares. The declining influence of domestic environment is further weakened by another tendency, prevalent almost everywhere today, which, under one pretext or another, for economic reasons, or for reasons of industry, trade, or politics, causes children to be more and more frequently sent away from home even in their tenderest years. . . .

*   *   *

. . . We implore pastors of souls . . . to warn Christian parents of their grave obligations. And this should be done not in a merely theoretical and general way, but with practical and specific application to the various responsibilities of parents touching the religious, moral, and civil training of their children, and with indication of the methods best adapted to make their training effective, supposing always the influence of their own exemplary lives. The Apostle of the Gentiles did not hesitate to descend to such details of practical instruction in his epistles, especially in the Epistle to the Ephesians, where among other things he gives this advice: "And you, fathers, provoke not your children to anger" (Eph. 6:4). This fault is the result not so much of excessive severity, as of impatience and of ignorance of means best calculated to effect a desired correction; it is also due to the all too common relaxation of parental discipline which fails to check the growth of evil passions in the hearts of the younger generation . . . [Pius XI, 1929, *Rappresentanti in Terra,* or *Divini Illius Magistri; SW,* II, 110–112].

Speaking about the Christian family as the stronghold of Christian life, Pius XII says:

In promoting this participation by the laity in the apostolate, which is so important in our times, the family has a special mission, for it is the spirit of the family that exercises the most powerful influence on that of the rising generation. As long as the sacred flame of the Faith burns on the domestic hearth, and the parents forge and fashion the lives of their children in accordance with this Faith, youth will be ever ready to acknowledge the royal prerogatives of the Redeemer, and to oppose those who wish to exclude Him from society or wrongly to usurp His rights.

When churches are closed, when the Image of the Crucified is taken from the schools, the family remains the providential and, in a certain sense, impregnable refuge of Christian life . . . [Pius XII, 1939, *Summi Pontificatus; CM,* XXXVII, 912].

Again he says:

With what solicitude do the parents take care that the children not only grow in physical vigor but also that, following in the footsteps of their forebears whose memory is often recalled to them, they may shine with the light which profession of the pure faith and moral goodness impart to them. Moved by the numerous benefits received, such children consider it their paramount duty to honor their parents, to be attentive to their desires, to be the staff of their old age, to rejoice their gray hairs with an affection which, unquenched by death, will be made more glorious and more complete in the mansion of Heaven.

The members of the Christian family, neither querulous in adversity nor ungrateful in prosperity, are ever filled with confidence in God to Whose will they acquiesce and upon Whose help they wait not in vain [Pius XII, 1939, *Sertum Laetitiae; CM,* XXXVII, 932].

To newlyweds, Pius XII said:

With love guided by reason and reason enlightened by faith, the home education will not be subject to those deplorable extremes that so often imperil: alternating weak indulgence with sharp severity, going from culpable acquiescence which leaves the child unguided, to severe correction that leaves him helpless. On the other hand the affection shown by parents to which there is a corresponding confidence on the part of the child, distributes with equal moderation, because it is master of itself, and with complete success because it has the child's love, due praise and merited correction. "Try to make yourself loved," St. John Bosco used to say, "and you will be obeyed" . . . [Pius XII, 1940, *Scritti e Discorsi*, II; *The Holy Father Speaks to Newlyweds*, p. 17].

Speaking about the harm of favoritism in the family, Pius XII says:

The whole education of your children would be ruined were they to discover in their parents — and their eyes are sharp enough to see — any signs of favoritism, undue preferences or antipathies in regard to any of them. For your own good and for the good of the family it must be clear that, whether you use measured severity or give encouragement and caresses, you have an equal love for all, a love which makes no distinction save for the correction of evil or for the encouragement of good. Have you not received them all equally from God? [Pius XII, 1941, *Women of Catholic Action; Clergy Review*, XXII, 137–138].

Benedict XV, writing about contempt of authority, states:

From the time when all human power sought to emancipate itself from God, the Creator and Father of the Universe, and to attribute its origin to man's free will, the bonds between superiors and inferiors have become so weak that they seem almost to have disappeared. An immoderate spirit of independence, combined with pride, has spread everywhere, invading even the family, whose authority so clearly arises from nature; and, what is more deplorable, it does not stop at the steps of the sanctuary . . . [Benedict XV, 1914, *Ad Beatissimi; CM*, XII, 737].

Benedict XV exhorts parents to train their children in the virtue of charity.

. . . We earnestly exhort all Christian parents, to whom the Heavenly Father has committed the grave charge of training to the practice of charity and the other virtues, to use this happy opportunity of exciting and cultivating in the minds of their children sentiments of humanity and holy compassion . . . [Benedict XV, 1920, *Annus Iam Plenus; CM,* XIX, 58].

FATHER AND THE FAMILY

Concerning the right and the responsibility of a father to provide for his family, Leo XIII writes:

For it is a most sacred law of nature that a father must provide food and all necessaries for those whom he has begotten. And, similarly, nature dictates that a man's children, who carry on, as it were, and continue his own personality, should be provided by him with all that is needful to enable them honourably to keep themselves from want and misery in the uncertainties of this mortal life . . . [Leo XIII, 1891, *Rerum Novarum; SW,* I, 173].

Pius XI writes:

And so, in the first place, every effort should be made to bring about that which Our predecessor Leo XIII, of happy memory, has already insisted upon, namely, that in the state such economic and social methods should be adopted as will enable every head of a family to earn as much as, according to his station in life, is necessary for himself, his wife, and for the rearing of his children, for "the laborer deserves his wages" (Lk. 10:7). To deny this, or to make light of what is equitable, is a grave injustice and is placed among the greatest sins by Holy Writ (Deut. 24:14, 15); nor is it lawful to fix such a scanty wage as will be insufficient for the upkeep of the family in the circumstances in which it is placed [Pius XI, 1930, CC; *SW,* II, 168–169].

About the workingman and his family, Pius XI states:

In the first place, the wage paid to the workingman must be sufficient for the support of himself and of his family. It is right indeed that the rest of the family contribute according to their power toward the common maintenance, as in the rural home or in the families of many artisans and small shopkeepers. . . .

*   *   *

Every effort must therefore be made that fathers of families receive a wage sufficient to meet adequately ordinary domestic needs. If in the present state of society this is not always feasible, social justice demands that reforms be introduced without delay which will guarantee every adult workingman just such a wage. In this connection We might utter a word of praise for the various systems devised and attempted in practice, by which an increased wage is paid in view of increased family burdens, and a special provision is made for special needs [Pius XI, 1931, *Quadragesimo Anno; SW*, II, 203].

Writing about justice and wages, Pius XII states:

. . . The salaries of the workers, as is just, are to be such that they are sufficient to maintain them and their families. Solemn are the words of Our predecessor, Pius XI, on this question:

"Every effort must therefore be made that fathers of families receive a wage sufficient to meet adequately normal domestic needs. If under present circumstances this is not always feasible, social justice demands that reforms be introduced without delay which will guarantee such a wage to every adult working man. In this connection We praise those who have most prudently and usefully attempted various methods by which an increased wage is paid in view of increased family burdens and special provision made for special needs" (Encyclical Letter *Quadragesimo Anno*).

May it also be brought about that each and every able-bodied man may receive an equal opportunity for work in order to earn the daily bread for himself and his own . . . [Pius XII, *Sertum Laetitiae; CM*, XXXVII, 936].

Referring to family support, the Holy Father says:

You are rightly solicitous for your daily bread and a suitable home which are indispensable for your maintenance and that of your families: see that this solicitude is not in conflict with your heavenly destiny. Let it not make you forgetful or neglectful of your soul and of the imperishable treasures which God has entrusted to you in the souls of your children.

Let it not obscure the vision or hinder the gaining of those eternal goods which will constitute your everlasting happiness and which become a reality in the supreme good for which we are created: our happiness in God . . . [Pius XII, 1949, *Christmas Message; CM,* XLVIII, 185].

In his discourse on adult education, Pius XII said:

As for the father of the family, one of his principal functions undoubtedly is to procure for his wife and children the financial means indispensable for life [Pius XII, 1953, *Discourse to the Pupils and Teachers for Adult Education; Catholic Documents,* No. 11, p. 25].

MOTHER AND THE FAMILY

Leo XIII writes:

. . . Women, again, are not suited to certain trades; for a woman is by nature fitted for homework, and it is that which is best adapted at once to preserve her modesty, and to promote the good bringing up of children and the well-being of the family [Leo XIII, 1891, *Rerum Novarum; SW,* I, 192].

Concerning modesty in dress, Benedict XV says to Catholic women:

. . . We rejoice at the resolution which has been formulated to secure that Catholic women, in addition to the duty of being modest, should also realize that of showing themselves such in manner of dress. . . .

* * *

It would be superfluous to say that a good mother must never permit her daughters to yield to false exigencies of a fashion which is not perfectly modest . . . [Benedict XV, 1919, Woman's Mission in Modern Society; *CM,* XVII, 454–455].

Again he says:

One cannot sufficiently deplore the blindness of so many women of every age and condition; made foolish by desire to please, they do not see to what a degree the indecency of their clothing shocks every honest man, and offends God [Benedict XV, 1921, *Sacra Propediem; CM,* XIX, 106].

Pius XI writes:

. . . Mothers will above all perform their work at home or near the home, giving their time to domestic cares. Intolerable, and to be opposed with all our strength, is the abuse whereby mothers of families, because of the insufficiency of the father's salary, are forced to engage in gainful occupations outside the domestic walls, to the neglect of their own proper cares and duties, particularly the education of their children [Pius XI, 1931, *Quadragesimo Anno; SW,* II, 203].

Pius XII, speaking about woman's natural sphere, says:

. . . Now the sphere of woman, her manner of life, her native bent, is motherhood. Every woman is made to be a mother: a mother in the physical meaning of the word or in the more spiritual and exalted but no less real sense.

For this purpose the Creator organized the whole characteristic make-up of woman, her organic construction, but even more her spirit, and above all her delicate sensitiveness. Thus it is that a woman who is a real woman can see all the problems of human life only in the perspective of the family. That is why her delicate sense of her dignity puts her on guard any time that a social or political order threatens to prejudice her mission as a mother or the good of the family [Pius XII, 1945, *Woman's Duties in Social and Political Life; CM,* XLIII, 708].

To the Congress of the International Union of Catholic Women's Leagues, Pius XII said:

. . . Most of you must continue to give the greater part of

your time and of your loving attention to the care of your homes and families. We must not forget that the making of a home in which all feel at ease and happy, and the bringing up of children are very special contributions to the common welfare. So we rejoice in the fact, which you yourselves rightly recorded, that among rural families, which are still such a large part of society, woman's work in the home still goes hand in hand with her contribution to the social and national economy [Pius XII, 1947, *Papal Directives for the Woman of Today; Catholic Action,* XXX, 19].

To the First Marian Congress of South Africa, Pius XII said:
. . . The home and civil society have felt the quickening pulse of a life purified by woman's love and holiness. Holiness and all that it implies of courage, self-restraint, patient endurance, kindliness, modesty, and unworldliness, how gracefully it becomes woman. It is the source of her greatest power for good . . . [Pius XII, 1952, *The Blessed Virgin Mary; CM,* LI, 128].

Speaking on adult education, Pius XII said:
. . . If the mother devotes herself to her mission as educator, giving suitable instruction and guidance, the life-cell of society will be healthy and strong. Mothers must acquire the elementary knowledge necessary for the government of the family, the art of keeping a house in order, of dealing with statements of accounting, useful ideas about bringing up children, and, above all, enough understanding of the rules of pedagogy, to profit by the experience of others, without placing too much confidence in their mother instinct, which, of itself, will not always and surely keep them from harmful mistakes [Pius XII, 1953, *Discourse to the Pupils and Teachers for Adult Education; Catholic Documents,* No. 11, 25–26].

On woman's absence from the home, Pius XII writes:
We see a woman who in order to augment her husband's earnings, betakes herself also to a factory, leaving her house abandoned during her absence. The house, untidy and small per-

haps before, becomes even more miserable for lack of care. Members of the family work separately in four quarters of the city and with different working hours. Scarcely ever do they find themselves together for dinner or rest after work — still less for prayer in common. What is left of family life? And what attractions can it offer to children?

*   *   *

To such painful consequences of the absence of the mother from the home there is added another, still more deplorable. It concerns the education, especially of the young girl, and her preparation for real life. Accustomed as she is to see her mother always out of the house and the house itself so gloomy in its abandonment, she will be unable to find any attraction for it, she will not feel the slightest inclination for austere housekeeping jobs. She cannot be expected to appreciate their nobility and beauty or to wish one day to give herself to them as a wife and mother.

This is true in all grades and stations of social life. The daughter of the worldly woman, who sees all housekeeping left in the hands of paid help and her mother fussing around with frivolous occupations and futile amusements, will follow her example, will want to be emancipated as soon as possible and in the words of a very tragic phrase "to live her own life." How could she conceive a desire to become one day a true lady that is the mother of a happy, prosperous, worthy family?

As to the working classes, forced to earn daily bread, a woman might, if she reflected, realize that not rarely the supplementary wage which she earns by working outside the house is easily swallowed up by the other expenses or even by waste which is ruinous to the family budget. . . .

*   *   *

It is clear that woman's task thus understood cannot be improvised. Motherly instinct is in her a human instinct, not determined by nature down to the details of its application. It is directed by free will and this in turn is guided by intellect. Hence comes its moral value and its dignity but also imperfection which must be compensated for and redeemed by education [Pius XII, 1945, *Woman's Duties in Social and Political Life; CM*, XLIII, 710, 714].

WOMAN IN PUBLIC LIFE

Concerning social action, Pius X writes:

. . . It is certain that the present constitution of States offers to all without distinction the power of influencing public opinion, and Catholics, while recognizing the obligations imposed by the law of God and the precepts of the Church, may with safe conscience enjoy this liberty, and prove themselves capable, as much as, and even more than others, of co-operating in the material and civil well-being of the people, thus acquiring that authority and respect which may make it even possible for them to defend and promote a higher good, namely, that of the soul.

These civil rights are many and various, going as far as a direct share in the political life of the country by representing the people in the legislature.

This makes it incumbent on all Catholics to prepare themselves prudently and seriously for political life in case they should be called to it. Hence it becomes necessary that this same activity, displayed by Catholics in preparing themselves by good electoral organization, for administrative life in parish and county councils, should be extended to a suitable preparation and organization for political life . . . [Pius X, 1905, *Il Fermo Proposito; The Pope and the People*, 1932 ed., pp. 196–197].

Benedict XV states that woman's apostolate has expanded, but that her natural center is still the family.

The changed conditions of the times have conferred upon woman functions and rights which were not allowed her in former times, but no change in the opinions of men, no novelty of circumstances and events, will ever remove woman, conscious of her mission, from her natural center, which is the family. At the domestic hearth she is queen. . . .

Hence, it may be justly said that the changed condition of the times have enlarged the field of woman's activity. An apostolate of woman in the world has succeeded that more intimate and restricted action which she formerly exercised within the domestic walls, but this apostolate must be carried out in such a manner as to make it evident that woman, both outside and within the home, shall not forget that it is her duty, even today, to consecrate her principal cares to the family [Benedict XV, 1919, *Woman's Mission in Modern Society; CM*, XVII, 453].

Pius XII tells the working women of Italy that industrial development has forced large numbers of women to work in factories and offices, but the home and the family must still be woman's first concern:
Woman is the heart of the family; the care of the home, in which she is queen, constitutes the center and *palestra* of her principal activity. But in this order of things, industry with its portentous progress has brought an unprecedented transformation in the history of human civic life. Industrial production, as you well know, has drawn to it a considerable part of domestic labors, appertaining to woman, and vice versa has obliged great multitudes of the feminine world to go out from the domestic hearth and devote their day's work in factories, in offices and on plantations. Not a few deplore such a change; but this is an accomplished fact, from which at present it is impossible to retreat.

*   *   *

For if you likewise, beloved daughters, must earn daily bread in factories, or on plantations, give to your husband and to your children, with redoubled fervor in the hours that you have left for the home, the exhortation of a good example, affectionate cares, constant love. See to it that your dwelling becomes, to use the expression of the Apostle Saint Paul, "a place of quiet and tranquil life, of all piety and dignity," always stirred by the resolution of assuring with conscious diligence to your family those healthy results, which the ancient Christian framework of customs, now abandoned, used to perform unconsciously. By keeping the holy days of obligation, devout attendance to the Holy Sacrifice of the Mass, frequency at the Eucharistic Table, you will attain courage in the profession of your faith, generous forbearance in the trials and tribulations of life, strength to keep purity of mind and habits, conjugal fidelity, maternal love ready for every renunciation, and above all the grace of Jesus which will abound in you, in your family, in your companions at work; so that rectitude and loyalty, respect for the right and dignity of others and the promptness of mutual aid may be the distinguishing qualities of your reciprocal relations.

*   *   *

. . . It is hardly necessary to remind you that, when it is a question of the fundamental morals of the family and the state, of the rights of God and of the Church, all, — men and women, — of whatever class and condition, are strictly obliged to make use of their political rights, in the service of a good cause [Pius XII, 1945, *To the Working Women of Italy; The Unwearied Advocate*, II, 35–37].

Concerning the duties of woman in social and political life, Pius XII said:

Let Us say at the outset that for Us the problem regarding woman, both in its entirety as a whole and in all its many details, resolves itself into preserving and augmenting that dignity which woman has had from God. . . .

*   *   *

Hence, it follows that those systems cannot treat the question of women's rights properly which exclude God and His law from the social life and give precepts of religion, at most, a lowly place in man's private life.

You, therefore, disregarding highsounding and empty slogans with which some people would qualify the movement for women's rights, have laudably organized and united as Catholic women and Catholic girls in order to meet in a becoming manner the natural needs and true interests of your sex.

*   *   *

In the face of theories and practice which by different ways are tearing a woman from her mission and, with a flattering promise of unbridled freedom or, in reality, of hopeless misery, are depriving her of her personal dignity, her dignity as woman, We have heard the cry of fear which calls for her active presence as far as possible in the home.

A woman is, in fact, kept out of the home not only by her so-called emancipation but often, too, by the necessities of life, by the continuous anxiety about daily bread. It would be useless then to preach to her to return to the home while conditions prevail which constrain her to remain away from it. And this brings Us to the first aspect of your mission in the social and political life which opens up before you.

Your entry into public life came about suddenly as a result of social upheavals which we see around us. It does not matter. You are called upon to take part. Will you, perhaps, leave (the responsibility) to others, to those who sponsor or collaborate in the ruin of some monopoly of social organization of which the family is the primary factor in its economic, juridical, spiritual and moral unity?

The fate of the family, the fate of human relations are at stake. They are in your hands. Every woman has then, mark it well, the obligation, the strict obligation in conscience, not to absent herself but to go into action in a manner and way suitable to the condition of each so as to hold back those currents which threaten the home, so as to oppose those doctrines which undermine its foundations, so as to prepare, organize and achieve its restoration.

To this powerful motive which impels a Catholic woman to enter upon a way that now is opened to her activity, there is added another, her dignity as a woman. She has to collaborate with man towards the good of the State in which she is of the same dignity as he. Each of the two sexes must take the part that belongs to it, according to its nature, special qualities, and physical, intellectual, and moral aptitude. Both have the right and duty to cooperate toward the total good of society and of their country.

* * *

. . . Let us take the case of civil rights: These are at present the same for both, but with how much more discernment and efficacy will they be utilized if man and woman come to complement one another. The sensitiveness and fine feeling proper to woman, which might lead her to judge by her impressions and would thus involve the risk of impeding clarity and breadth of vision, serenity of judgment and forethought for remote consequences, are, on the contrary, of immense help when it is a question of throwing light on the needs, aspirations and dangers that touch domestic, public welfare or religious spheres.

. . . It is a vast field of activity which now lies open to woman and it can be corresponding to the mentality of character of each, either intellectual or actively practical. To study and expound the place and role of woman in society, her rights and duties; to become a teacher-guide to one's sisters and to direct ideas, dissipate prejudices, clarify obscure points, explain and diffuse the teachings of the Church in order more securely to discredit error, illusion and falsehood, in order to express more effectively the tactics of those who oppose Catholic dogma and morals — is an immense work and one of impelling necessity, without which all the zeal of the Apostolate could obtain but precarious results. But direct action, too, is indispensable if we do not want the same doctrines and solid convictions to remain, if not entirely of academic interest, at least of little practical consequence.

This direct participation, this effective collaboration in social and political activity does not at all change the normal activity of woman. Associated with men in civil institutions, she will apply herself especially to those matters which call for tact, delicacy and maternal instinct rather than administrative rigidity. Who better than she can understand what is needed for the dignity of woman, the integrity and honor of the young girl, and the protection and education of the child?

And in all these questions, how many problems call for study and action on the part of governments and legislators. Only a woman will know, for instance, how to temper with kindness, without detriment to its efficacy, legislation to repress licentiousness. She alone can find the means to save from degradation and to raise in honesty and in religious and civil virtues the morally derelict young. She alone will be able to render effective the work of protection and rehabilitation for those freed from prison and for fallen girls. She alone will re-echo from her own heart the plea of mothers from whom the totalitarian state, by whatever name it be called, would will to snatch the education of their children.

*   *   *

But in your social and political activity much depends on the legislation of the State and the administration of local bodies. Accordingly, the electoral ballot in the hands of Catholic woman is an important means toward the fulfillment of her strict duty in conscience, especially at the present time. The State and politics have, in fact, precisely the office of securing for the family or every social class conditions necessary for them to exist and to evolve as economic, juridical and moral units. Then the family will really be the vital nucleus of men who are earning honestly their temporal and eternal welfare.

. . . No wise woman favors a policy of class struggle or war. Her vote is a vote for peace . . . [Pius XII, 1945, *Woman's Duties in Social and Political Life; CM,* XLIII, 705, 711–715].

To the Congress of the International Union of Catholic Women's leagues, Pius XII said:

Catholic women and girls, formerly you would have thought only of worthily playing your sacred and fruitful role in the management of a wholesome, strong, and radiant home; or you would have consecrated your life to the service of God in the composure of the cloister or in apostolic and charitable works. But now you appear abroad, you enter the arena to take part in the battle: you have not sought to do so, but courageously you accept your new duties; not as resigned victims nor merely in a defensive spirit; you are determined to pass to the counter-attack and conquer.

Such is the thought which emerges from the substantial documents, in which your programs of action are set forth, and in which are clearly drawn the lines of discussion of your present congress. This rich documentation reflects, as in a mirror, the actual situation — one must say, alas, the actual drama of woman's world. Towards the center converge all the rays of activity of woman in her social and political life, an activity of which the object is above all else, to protect the dignity of the daughter, of the wife, of the mother; to preserve the home, the family, the child in their primordial order; to safeguard the rights of the family, and make all efforts bear toward the safekeeping of the child under the guardianship of his parents.

*   *   *

There remains to be considered the domain of political life. . . . This domain has several distinct aspects: the safeguard and care of the sacred interests of woman, by means of legislation and administration that respects her rights, dignity, and social function — the participation of some women in political life for the good, the welfare, and the progress of all.

Your own role is, in general, to work toward making woman always more conscious of her sacred rights, of her duties, and of her power to help mold public opinion, through her daily contacts, and to influence legislation and administration by the proper use of her prerogatives as citizen. Such is your common role. It does not mean that you are all to have political careers as members of public assemblies. . . .

*   *   *

Those among you who have more leisure and are suitably prepared, will take up the burden of public life and be, as it were, your delegated representatives. Give them your confidence, understand their difficulties, the hard work and sacrifices their devotion entails; give them your help and support [Pius XII, 1947, *Papal Directives for the Woman of Today; Catholic Action*, XXX, 17, 19].

CHILD AND THE FAMILY

Speaking about reciprocal family duties, Leo XIII says:

. . . Hence the Apostle exhorts children to "obey their parents in the Lord, and honour their father and mother, which is the first commandment with promise" (Eph. 6:1, 2) . . . [Leo XIII, 1878, *Quod Apostolici Muneris; SW,* I, 20].

Treating about paternal authority, the same pope writes:

Paternal authority can neither be abolished by the State nor absorbed; for it has the same source as human life itself. "Children are in some way part of the father," and as it were, the continuation of the father's personality. Strictly speaking, the child takes its place in civil society not in its own right, but in its quality as member of the family in which it is begotten. And it is precisely because "the child belongs to the father," that "before it attains the use of free will, it is in the power and care of its parents" (St. Thomas, 2a, 2ae, q. x, a. 12). Socialists, therefore, in setting aside the parent and introducing the providence of the State, act against natural justice, and threaten the very existence of family life [Leo XIII, 1891, *Rerum Novarum; SW,* I, 174–175].

On child labor, Leo XIII writes:

. . . In regard to children, great care should be taken not to place them in workshops and factories until their bodies and minds are sufficiently mature. For just as rough weather destroys the buds of spring, so too early an experience of life's hard work blights the young promise of a child's powers, and makes any real education impossible . . . [Leo XIII, 1891, *Rerum Novarum; SW,* I, 192].

Concerning the ideal Christian home, Pius XI writes:

. . . In an ideal home the parents, like Tobias and Sara, beg of God a numerous posterity "in which Thy name may be blessed forever," and receive it as a gift from heaven and a precious trust (Tob. 8:9). They strive to instill into their children from their early years a holy fear of God, and true Christian piety; they foster a tender devotion to Jesus, the Blessed Sacrament, and the Immaculate Virgin; they teach respect and veneration for holy places and persons. In such a home the children see in their parents a model of an upright, industrious, and pious life; they see their parents holily loving each other in our Lord, see them approach the holy sacraments frequently and not only obey the laws of the Church concerning abstinence and fasting, but observe the spirit of voluntary Christian mortification; they see them pray at home, gathering around them all the family, that common prayer may rise more acceptably to heaven; they find them compassionate toward the distress of others and see them divide with the poor the much or the little they possess [Pius XI, 1935, *Ad Catholici Sacerdotii; SW*, II, 428].

Concerning the care of old people, Pius XII said to newlyweds: The old people! One is sometimes, perhaps unconsciously, annoyed by their little wants and their innocent complaints; there are wrinkles that time has dug into their souls, like those that furrow their brows, but these should make them all the more worthy of respect. . . . Toward these, regardless of your own age, you are bound, as you know, by the precept of the Decalogue, "Honor thy father and thy mother" (Exod. 20:12). You will not be of the number of those ungrateful children who neglect their old parents, and who in turn will, often enough, find themselves abandoned when age renders them in need of assistance [Pius XII, 1940, *Scritti e Discorsi*, II; *The Holy Father Speaks to Newlyweds*, p. 40].

About the daughter who goes out to work, Pius XII says: . . . The daughter who also goes out to work in a factory or office, deafened by the excited restless world in which she lives, dazzled by the tinsel of specious luxury, developing a thirst for shallow pleasures . . . in those revue or dance halls which are sprouting up everywhere, often for party propaganda purposes, and which corrupt youth, becomes a fashionable lady, despises the old Nineteenth Century ways of life.

How could she not feel her modest home surroundings unattractive and more squalid than they were in reality? To find her pleasure in them, to desire one day to settle in them herself, she should be able to offset her natural impressions by a serious intellectual and spiritual life, by the vigor that comes from religious education and from the supernatural ideals. But what kind of formation has she received in such surroundings?

And that is not all. When, as the years pass, her mother prematurely aged, worn out, and broken by work beyond her capacity, by sorrow and anxiety, will see her return home at night at a very late hour, she will not find her a support or a help but rather the mother herself will have to wait on a daughter incapable and unaccustomed to household work and to perform for her all the offices of a servant.

And the lot of the father will not be any better when old age, sickness, infirmity and unemployment force him to depend for his meager sustenance on the good or bad will of his children. Here you have the august holy authority of the father and mother dethroned [Pius XII, 1945, *Woman's Duties in Social and Political Life; CM*, XLIII, 710].

Something can be done for the girl who has to work outside of the home, says Pius XII.

. . . It is possible to supply, at least in part, for this deficiency by securing for the young girl who of necessity must work outside of the home one of those occupations which are, to some extent, a training ground and a noviceship for the life for which she is destined. To such a purpose also serve those schools of domestic economy which aim at making of the child and the young girl of today the wife and mother of tomorrow.

How worthy of praise and encouragement are such institutions! . . . [Pius XII, 1945, *Woman's Duties in Social and Political life; CM*, XLIII, 714].

Pius XII states that the daughter should receive proper training under the direction of her mother.

Education proper to her sex of the young girl, and not rarely also of the grown woman, is therefore a necessary condition of her preparation and formation for a life worthy of her. The ideal would evidently be that this education should begin with infancy in the intimacy of the Catholic home under the direction of the mother . . . [Pius XII, 1945, *Woman's Duties in Social and Political Life; CM*, XLIII, 714].

About the bachelor girl, Pius XII writes:

. . . But the young Catholic girl, too, who remains unmarried perforce, trusting nonetheless the providence of our Heavenly Father, recognizes in the vicissitudes of life the call of the Master: The Master is come and calleth for thee (Jn. 11:28). She hearkens. She gives up the fond dream of her adolescence and youth to have a faithful companion in life and set up a family. And in the exclusion of Matrimony she recognizes her vocation. Then, with a sorrowful but submissive heart, she too gives herself up to the noble and most diversified good works [Pius XII, 1945, *Woman's Duties in Social and Political Life; CM*, XLIII, 708].

FAMILY AND THE ECONOMIC SITUATION

Leo XIII states that the State must aid and protect the family, but it must go no further.

The idea . . . that the civil government should, at its own discretion, penetrate and pervade the family and the household, is a great and pernicious mistake. True, if a family finds itself in great difficulty, utterly friendless, and without prospect of help, it is right that extreme necessity be met by public aid; for each family is a part of the commonwealth . . . [Leo XIII, 1891, *Rerum Novarum; SW*, I, 174].

Writing about distributive justice, Leo XIII states:

. . . The poor are members of the national community equally with the rich; they are real component parts, living parts, which make up, through the family, the living body; and it need hardly be said that they are by far the majority. It would be irrational to neglect one portion of the citizens and to favour another; and therefore the public administration must duly and solicitously provide for the welfare and the comfort of the working people, or else that law of justice will be violated which ordains that each shall have his due. . . . [Leo XIII, 1891, *Rerum Novarum; SW,* I, 186].

State aid should be given to families in need, says Pius XI.

If, however, for this purpose, private resources do not suffice, it is the duty of the public authority to supply for the insufficient forces of individual effort, particularly in a matter which is of such importance to the commonweal, touching as it does the maintenance of the family and married people. If families, particularly those in which there are many children, have not suitable dwellings; if the husband cannot find employment and means of livelihood; if the necessities of life cannot be purchased except at exorbitant prices; if even the mother of the family to the great harm of the home, is compelled to go forth and seek a living by her own labors; if she, too, in the ordinary or even extraordinary labors of childbirth, is deprived of proper food, medicine, and the assistance of a skilled physician, it is patent to all to what an extent married people may lose heart, and how home life and the observance of God's commands are rendered difficult for them. Indeed it is obvious how great a peril can arise to the public security and to the welfare and very life of civil society itself when such men are reduced to such a condition of desperation that, having nothing which they fear to lose, they are emboldened to hope for chance advantage from the upheaval of the state and of established order.

Wherefore, those who have the care of the state and of the public good cannot neglect the needs of married people and their families, without bringing great harm upon the state and on the common welfare. Hence, in making the laws and in disposing of public funds they must do their utmost to relieve the needs of the poor, considering such a task as one of the most important of their administrative duties [Pius XI, 1930, CC; *SW,* II, 169–170].

Deploring the poverty of some families, Pius XII says:

Now our thoughts turn with special affectionate concern to the suffering army of the poor, scattered throughout the world. . . . Before the mind's eyes pass those families over whom hangs, like a menacing spectre, the danger of being cut off from the source of all livelihood by sudden unemployment. . . . And what is to be said of those families who have some little work, but no home, and live in temporary barracks, in caves which would not be given to animals?

But the most desolate picture is presented by families who have simply nothing. These are families in "utter wretchedness": the father without work, the mother watching her children wasting away, absolutely impotent to help them. Never is there bread, never are there enough clothes to cover them, and woe to the whole family when sickness makes its dread visitation to that cave now become a human habitation.

Whole masses of population are brought up as enemies of law and order, so many poor girls gone astray, pushed down into the bottom of the abyss, because they believed that that was the only way out of their shameful poverty . . . [Pius XII, 1952, *Christmas Eve Address; CM*, LI, 119].

To the Catholic International Congress for Social Study, Pius XII said:

The time has come to face squarely, in its full dimension, the duty of providing for countless families, in their natural, moral, juridical and economic unity a just living-space which meets, however modestly but at the very least in sufficient measure, the demands of human dignity . . . [Pius XII, 1950, *Production of Human Needs; CM*, XLVIII, 507].

Concerning the influence of the technological spirit on modern men's lives, Pius XII writes:

. . . Wherever technology reigns supreme, there human society will be transformed into a colorless mass, into something impersonal and without substance, and this contrary to the clear designs of nature and of the Creator.

And with particular anxiety We consider the danger threatening the family, which is the strongest principle of order in society. For the family is capable of inspiring in its members innumerable daily acts of service, binds them to the home and hearth with the bonds of affection, and awakes in each of them a love of the family traditions in the production and conservation of useful goods. Wherever on the contrary the technological concept of life penetrates, the family loses its personal bond of unity, is deprived of its warmth and stability. It remains united only to the extent that is demanded by the exigencies of mass production, which is being pursued with more and more insistence. No longer is the family a work of love and a haven for souls; it is rather a desolate depot, according to the circumstances, either of manpower for mass production, or of consumers of the material goods produced [Pius XII, 1953, *Christmas Message; CM*, LII, 179].

Concerning the role of family saving, Pius XII states:
Indeed, the habit and practice of thrift has . . . significance. . . .
Who can doubt that such a manner of life notably contributes to maintain in a family a spirit of unity and a spirit of joy, amid a serene simplicity, and moral dignity? Not at all desirous of searching outside for costly diversions, which leave behind only a bitter taste, father, mother and children know how to find healthy satisfactions among themselves, in their own home or in the restricted circle of their friends. Such a home, where every evening each one has a keen desire to be, after the work and fatigue and troubles of the day, is loved, and all the members of the family take care of it as a sanctuary, and each one, according to his special aptitude and his personal capacity, strives to embellish it and make order and joy reign within . . . [Pius XII, 1950, *The Role of Family Saving; CM*, XLIX, 330–331].

FAMILY AND WAR

War helps to break up families, says Pius XI.
. . . The breaking up of the family by this, already begun

at an earlier time, has been much accentuated by the great war, leading as it did to the dispersion of fathers and sons to distant lands and the widespread increase of moral corruption. So it has come to pass that paternal authority is no longer in honor, that ties of friendship have been relaxed, that masters and servants are at strife, that the bond of marriage itself is but too often violated, and that married people have come to neglect their sacred duties toward God and civil society [Pius XI, 1922, *Ubi Arcano; SW*, II, 8].

In a radio message to the Spanish people, Pius XII said:
We cannot conceal the bitter pain which We experience at the record of so many innocent little children removed from their families and taken to strange countries with so much danger of apostasy and perversion, and We desire nothing more ardently than to see them restored to the love of their own families . . . [Pius XII, 1939, *Message Broadcast to Spain; The Pope Speaks,* 1940 ed., p. 136].

Referring to the calamity of war, Pius XII says:
But see how today, in the whirlwind of war, the vigor and beauty of so much of your youth, developed and perfected on fields of sport, declines or loses its burnish in the military hospital, while many young people wander physically and morally mutilated or unfit, through the thoroughfares of their native land, which, in the cities of some of its finest regions, has been reduced to a heap of ruins by aerial bombardment and by military operations.

If a section of the young men have no longer energy to labor and work, the mothers-to-be of the next generation, forced as they are to do straining work beyond all measure and time limit, are losing the possibility of giving to a people bled white that healthy increase of body and spirit which promotes the life and education of those children without whom the future of their native land is threatened with a tragic eclipse.

The painful irregularity of work and of a life far from God and from His grace, seduced and misguided by bad example, induces and facilitates a harmful relaxation of marriage and family relations so that the poison of lust tends now to defile, much more than heretofore, the sacred wells of life. From these sad facts and dangerous tendencies it appears unfortunately evident that, although the strengthening of the family and of the people was considered by many nations one of their noblest aims, there is growing and spreading now, instead, a physical deterioration and moral perversion which can be cured in part, only after many generations of a process of healing and preventive education [Pius XII, 1943, *Christmas Message; CM*, XLII, 69–70].

To the Association of Large Families, Pius XII said:
. . . The damages caused by the First World War were far from having been fully repaired when the second even more terrible conflagration came to augment them. Much time will be needed yet, and many labours on the part of men, with even greater divine aid, before the deep wound inflicted on the family by two wars can begin to heal properly. Another evil, partly due to these devastating conflicts, but also a consequence of over-population and of various unsuitable or selfish tendencies, is the housing crisis. All those who endeavor to remedy this evil, be they legislators, statesmen or social workers, perform, even if only in an indirect way, an apostolate of eminent worth. The same holds as regards combatting the scourge of unemployment, and providing for a sufficient family wage so that the mother will not be obliged — as too often happens — to seek employment outside the home but may be able to dedicate herself more to her husband and her children . . . [Pius XII, 1951, *Morality in Marriage; CM*, L, 307].

FAMILY UNDER COMMUNISM

Concerning the family under communism, Pius XI has this to say:
Refusing to human life any sacred or spiritual character, such a doctrine logically makes of marriage and the family a purely

artificial and civil institution, the outcome of a specific economic system. There exists no matrimonial bond of a juridico-moral nature that is not subject to the whim of the individual or of the collectivity. Naturally, therefore, the notion of an indissoluble marriage tie is scouted. Communism is particularly characterized by the rejection of any link that binds woman to the family and the home, and her emancipation is proclaimed as a basic principle. She is withdrawn from the family and the care of her children, to be thrust, instead, into public life and collective production under the same conditions as man. The care of home and children then devolves upon the collectivity [Pius XI, 1937, *Divini Redemptoris; SW*, II, 345].

FAMILY AND MOVIES

Movies can have an evil influence on the family, but also a good and wholesome influence, says Pius XI.

Everyone knows what damage is done to the soul by bad motion pictures. They are occasions of sin; they seduce young people along the ways of evil by glorifying the passions; they show life under a false light; they cloud ideals; they destroy pure love, respect for marriage, and affection for the family. They are capable also of creating prejudices among individuals, misunderstandings among nations, among social classes, and among entire races.

On the other hand, good motion pictures are capable of exercising a profoundly moral influence upon those who see them.

*   *   *

It is most necessary, therefore, in these our times to watch and strive to the end that the motion picture may no longer be made a school of corruption, but that it be transformed into an effectual means for the education and elevation of mankind.

And here we record with pleasure that high public officials, concerned at the influence exercised by the cinema in the moral and educational fields, have instituted select committees constituted of upright and honest persons, especially fathers and mothers of families, to inspect, censor, and direct the films to be published [Pius XI, 1936, *Vigilanti Cura; SW,* II, 309–311].

Concerning the perils of youth, Pius XI writes:
. . . We know to how many perils the children and youth are exposed, today more than ever. This is true everywhere, but particularly in Mexico, where an immoral and antireligious press implants in their hearts the seed of apostasy from Jesus Christ. To remedy such grave evil and defend your youth from these perils, it is necessary that every legal means be taken and every form of organization be put in motion, as for example, the Leagues of Fathers of Families, and the morality and vigilance committees for publications and censorship of the cinema [Pius XI, 1937, *Firmissimam Constantiam; SW,* II, 384].

About the influence of Motion Pictures Pius XII has this to say:
One wonders at times if the leaders of the Motion Picture Industries fully appreciate the vast power they wield in affecting social life, whether in the family or the larger civic groups. The eyes and ears are like broad avenues that lead directly to the soul of man; and they are opened wide, most often without challenge, by the spectators of your films. What is it that enters from the screen into the inner recesses of the mind, where youth's fund of knowledge is growing and norms and motives of conduct, which will mould the definite character, are being shaped and sharpened? Is it something that will make for a better citizen, industrious, law-abiding, God-fearing, who finds his joy and recreation in wholesome pleasure and fun? St. Paul was quoting Menander, an ancient Greek poet, when he wrote to the faithful of his church in Corinth, that "bad conversation corrupts good manners" (1 Cor. 15:33). What was true then, is no less true today; because human nature changes little with the centuries. And if it is true, as it is, that bad conversation corrupts morals, how much more effectively are they corrupted by bad conversation when accompanied by conduct, vividly depicted,

which flouts the laws of God and civilized decency? Oh, the immense amount of good the motion picture can effect! That is why the evil spirit, always so active in this world, wishes to pervert this instrument for his own impious purposes; and it is encouraging to know that your committee is aware of the danger, and more and more conscious of its grave responsibility before society and God. It is for public opinion to sustain wholeheartedly and effectively every legitimate effort made by men of integrity and honour to purify the films and keep them clean, to improve them and increase their usefulness [Pius XII, 1945, *Responsibility of the Motion Picture Industry; The Unwearied Advocate*, II, 32–33].

FAMILY RITUAL

Pope Pius XI states that parents should lead their children in the recitation of the Holy Rosary, every day, without exception.

And in this matter let fathers and mothers of families especially be an example to their offspring. When at the end of day all have returned home from their work and their business, let them kneel before an image of our heavenly Mother, and with one voice, one faith, one mind, let the parents lead their children in the recitation of the Holy Rosary. This is a beautiful and salutary custom from which the family circle cannot but draw peace and tranquillity, and obtain heavenly gifts. When, therefore, on frequent occasions, We receive newly married couples in audience and address paternal words to them, we give them rosaries, earnestly recommending the recitation of the beads, citing Our own example, that they may never one single day omit this practice, no matter how burdened they may be with cares and labor [Pius XI, 1937, *Ingravescentibus Malis; SW*, II, 396–397].

Concerning devotion to the Sacred Heart, Pius XII said to newlyweds:

. . . To be at the school of Jesus and to learn from His

Heart gentleness and humility, the divine remedies for violence and pride, whence all the faults and misfortunes of man proceed (Ecclus. 10:15), is the way of peace for individuals as well as for nations. It shall be for you, also the source of the happiness you desire and which We wish for your family.

It is fitting then, dear Christian husbands and wives, brethren of Jesus, that the image of His Heart "which has so loved men," be exposed and honored in your homes, like that of the nearest and most loved relation who pours out the treasures of His blessings upon you, your children, and your undertakings. . . . This image should not only watch over your hours of rest in a private chamber, but it should be loyally honored by being hung above the entrance, or in the dining room, or parlor, or in some other frequently used place. . . .

*   *   *

In a word, the Sacred Heart is duly honored in a home when He is acknowledged as the King of love by each and every one; which is to say that the family is consecrated to Him, inasmuch as the total giving of oneself to a holy cause or a holy person is called consecration. . . .

*   *   *

Make this Heart the king of your home and you will assure its peace; particularly since, renewing and determining the blessings of His Heavenly Father granted to faithful families, He has promised that peace shall reign in those families consecrated to Him [Pius XII, 1940, *Scritti e Discorsi*, II; *The Holy Father Speaks to Newlyweds*, pp. 27–28, 34].

In regard to prayer and recreation, Pius XII said:
. . . There are young men who think that, beginning at a certain age, prayer is like incense whose sweet smoke, like perfume, is better left to women. Others go to Mass now and then when they find it convenient, but they believe, as it would seem, that they are too grown up to kneel, and not mystical enough, as some say, to approach Holy Communion. Nor are there wanting young women, who, though carefully brought up by

their mothers and the good Sisters, believe that once they are married they are exempt from the most elementary laws of prudence, that dangerous reading, shows, dances, and recreations are all permitted them.

*   *   *

On the other hand, in a truly Christian family, the husband knows that his soul is of the same nature and not stronger than that of his wife and his children; hence he unites his daily prayers with theirs . . . [Pius XII, 1940, *Scritti e Discorsi*, II; *The Holy Father Speaks to Newlyweds*, p. 44].

The family should be born again and find new life through the Holy Eucharist, Pius XII stated.

. . . Husband and wife, parents and children: mystery of love on earth! The Eucharist: mystery of love divine, which sustains and perfects the spiritual life, and makes the family flourish as a garden of God's choice. . . .

. . . For where can fathers better betake themselves to find the gifts of understanding, prudence and self-forgetfulness which their mission as educators demands? Whence shall the spirit of their sons draw the most orderly and complete development? . . . Do you look for children docile, humble and obedient? In the Eucharist there is present the same Incarnate God Who "advanced in wisdom and age and grace with God and men" (Luke 11:52). Do you wish them to be noble in spirit and lofty in ideal? The Eucharist has all the allurement of divine tenderness and shows in clear light the unspeakable designs of the Redeemer.

It is, in truth, through the Holy Eucharist that the Church desires that the family, which is the living cell of society, and of the Church, should be born again and find new life. In its turn the family will thus become a centre of attraction for the fragrance that proceeds from the Eucharist, linking the sweetest things in home life with the most holy Sacrament [Pius XII, 1949, *Eucharistic Congress at Cali in Colombia; Catholic Documents.* No. II, 2].

The family rosary brings many blessings, says Pius XII.

. . . It is above all in the bosom of the family that We desire the custom of the Holy Rosary to be everywhere adopted, religiously preserved, and ever more intensely practiced. . . .

*   *   *

. . . What a sweet sight — most pleasing to God — when, at eventide, the Christian home resounds with the frequent repetition of praises in honor of the august Queen of Heaven! Then the Rosary, recited in common, assembles before the image of the Virgin, in an admirable union of hearts, the parents and their children, who come back from their daily work. . . .

. . . It links all more lightly in a sweet bond of love, with the most Holy Virgin, who, like a loving mother, in the circle of her children, will be there bestowing upon them an abundance of the gifts of concord and family peace [Pius XII, 1951, *Ingruentium Malorum; CM,* XLIX, 828].

In a radio message, Pius XII said to Austrian Catholics:

. . . Sacred to you all must be family prayer and the Christian Sunday. It should and must remain the Lord's day, the day of spiritual and physical rest, the day of joy for the family . . . [Pius XII, 1952, *To Austrian Catholics; CM,* LI, 50].

RURAL FAMILY

In a radio address to the German Catholic Congress, Bochum, Pius XII said:

. . . The first is the Christian life of the family. Wherever this still remains, principally in rural districts, preserve and defend it. Yes, defend it, because even there it is in danger of being lost . . . [Pius XII, 1949, *The Social Problems; CM,* XLVII, 708].

To the members of the International Catholic Congress on Rural Problems, Pius XII said:

. . . We are thinking first of the peasant farm, of the family-type farm. . . . No other working group is so suited as this to the life of the family, viewed as a spiritual, economic and juridical unit . . . [Pius XII, 1951, *Problems of Rural Life; CM,* XLIX, 710].

URBAN FAMILY

To German Catholics, Pius XII said:
. . . The first is the Christian life of .the family. . . . Where it has already disappeared, particularly in some urban working-class districts, rebuild it. You cannot give to your children and your young people anything more precious than the Christian life and perfection of the family [Pius XII, 1949, *The Social Problems; CM,* XLVII, 704].

Conclusion

ASPECTS OF MARRIAGE AND THE FAMILY
STRESSED BY THE POPES: 1878–1954

In general it can be said that there is little really new in the pronouncements of the popes on marriage and the family during the past three quarters of a century. A few questions were posed for the first time: e.g., the possibility of artificial insemination. Contraception practices became a serious matter, but the idea is very old and the Church's answer had been given long ago. The gradual replacement of the patriarchal type family with a more democratic type did not call for any modification of Church doctrine, although the extreme views once fully expressed by modern advocates of freedom had to be corrected. Perhaps the most significant development was the changing status of woman in the social, economic, and political spheres. The popes' position here was one of caution, warning against excesses, while granting woman's social mission had expanded and that custom and law allowed modern women a wider sphere of activity in public life. The paternal guidance of the popes directed women to use the new opportunities of influence for the good of the family and public morality, but not to the detriment of prior responsibilities to home and family.

LEO XIII (1878–1903)

Leo XIII's writings on marriage and the family are primarily a restatement of traditional Catholic doctrine and a defense of that doctrine against the materialistic and secularistic philosophy of his day, a philosophy strongly influenced by the heresies of dialectical materialism and Rousseau's naturalism. This philosophy as applied to the family not only rejected any claim of the Church to regulate marriage, it made marriage a purely private agreement between two individuals.

In answering, Leo reviewed the history of the family from the beginning, as recorded in Genesis, through Biblical times, the Greco-Roman period, and the Christian centuries. He shows that marriage was originally considered as ordained by God, a holy thing and not a purely secular institution. He shows that it was afterward corrupted, as in the pagan cultures of Greece and Rome, and partly so even by the Jews when divorce was allowed. But it was restored to its pristine status by Christ, who reminded the Jews that marriage was made by God in Paradise and stressed its unity and indissolubility. He went even further and elevated matrimony to the dignity of a sacrament, so that it became for husband and wife a major means of attaining personal holiness.

In making marriage a sacrament, Christ committed the regulation and defense of marriage to the Church. In turn, the Church, even during the first centuries of her existence, successfully defended the Christian teachings concerning marriage against the systems of "free love" advocated by the Gnostics, Manicheans, and Montanists. Further, the Church always exercised her authority in matters pertaining to marriage, and it was largely due to her that slaves were recognized as having the same natural right to marry as free men; that the double code of morality in favor of the male sex was originally rejected in Western culture; that the rights of parents were limited when it was a matter of their children marrying freely whom they chose. In fact, the regulation of marriage was often a means of protecting and preserving healthy family life as is illustrated by ecclesiastical impediments.

Leo reminds the State that all marriages are sacred, even those of unbelievers, while purely civil marriages among Christians attempt to deny the Church her Christ-given power concerning matrimonial unions. He warns that no power can dissolve a Christian marriage which has been ratified and consummated and that allowing divorce leads to a desecration of marriage. In defending the rights of the family against State intervention he emphasizes the need of parental authority, the right of parents to care for and educate their children, the right of the head of the family to a decent opportunity to support the family. It is only under certain specific circumstances that State intervention in the family is justified. On the other hand the State would make a real contribution to family life and its own welfare if it would co-operate with the Church in defending the teachings of Christ concerning marriage and facilitate to the extent possible the observance of these teachings by its citizens.

PIUS X (1903–1914)

Pius X was primarily concerned with such ecclesiastical matters as Church music, the Divine Office, Canon Law, and Biblical studies. But above all he had at heart the purity of the faith and spent much time in pointing out the dangers in what came to be known as Modernism. It was in connection with his disciplinary and legal work that the Sacred Congregation issued, with his authority, the "Decree Concerning Sponsalia and Matrimony" (August 2, 1907), a decree which specified the manner and the conditions under which Catholic marriages were to take place.

BENEDICT XV (1914–1922)

World War I, 1914–1918, had just begun when Benedict XV was elected Pope, and his untiring preoccupation was perforce to re-establish peace among the warring nations. He did call attention to the fact that the growing contempt for authority was penetrating even family life; and he deplored the growing lack of modesty among women. Most significant, however, was his noting the expanding field of women's activity both in civil society and in the lay apostolate and thus initiating what might be called a re-evaluation of the place of woman in modern society.

PIUS XI (1922–1939)

The great encyclical on marriage of Leo XIII (*Arcanum*, 1880) and that of Pius XI (*Casti Connubii*, 1930) appeared just fifty years apart. Much had happened meanwhile as is evident from the events referred to under the last three preceding popes. In addition, a world war left Europe prostrate, atheistic communism secured a foothold in Russia, the feminist movement gained adherents in a number of countries, and the Roman Question was settled by the Lateran Treaty (1929) which freed Pius' energies for wider fields. The versatility of Pius XI soon became evident. To the *Arcanum* of Leo he added one of the greatest of all encyclicals, *Casti Connubii*.

Pius XI states that his encyclical on marriage and the family is a supplement to Leo's encyclical on Christian marriage. Like Leo, he emphasizes the divine origin of marriage, the fact that it is a great sacrament of the New Law, and that each marriage arises only from the free consent of each of the spouses.

Following the classical scheme of St. Augustine, Pius divides his analysis into three parts. First, he speaks about the child, its need of being cared for and educated in a religious atmosphere. Secondly, he treats about mutual faithfulness with all its ramifications: monogamy, conjugal fidelity, chastity, and the status of husband and wife in the family; he says the husband is the head of the family, and the wife he calls the heart and the queen of the family. Thirdly, he speaks of the sacrament, which implies indissolubility of marriage, the dignity of marriage, and a sacred nuptial union, perfected by God's grace.

Like Leo, Pius aimed at combating the fallacious ideas about marriage current at his time: civil divorce, birth control, abortion, eugenics, sterilization, companionate marriage, and the false emancipation of woman. Thus he stresses the divine institution, the unity of marriage, the sacredness of the sacrament, conjugal fidelity, and the natural rights of individuals. In strongest terms he denounces artificial contraception and abortion as debasing and as contrary to the natural and divine law.

Pius XI discourages mixed marriages and bemoans the modern substitution of a certain vague compatibility of temperament for true and solid love which is the basis of conjugal happiness. He states that happiness in marriage is consequent upon knowledge of the basic Catholic doctrines of marriage, the wise choice of a marriage partner, co-operation of husband and wife, submission to the laws of God and His Church, and co-operation with God's grace.

He defends the right of the family to educate and to care for their offspring; he stresses the need of religious training, character formation, and sex instruction. Atheistic communism, he says, makes Christian family life impossible, and he pleads with civil authorities to help the Church to enforce what is prescribed by divine and ecclesiastical law concerning nuptial unions.

He states that the father of a family has the right and the obligation to support himself, his wife, and his children in a decent manner.

PIUS XII (1939–   )

World War II broke out within six months of Pius XII's coronation and the world struggle preoccupied his time for the next six years; nevertheless, in his public documents he touched on nearly every phase of marriage and the family. He wrote about the sacrament of marriage, the evils of mixed marriages, the invalidity of civil marriages of Catholics, the menace of civil divorce, the harmful effects of war on family life, and he mentioned the fact, as did Leo, that non-Christian marriages are less stable than Christian marriages.

Perhaps the most important pronouncements on marriage and the family by Pius XII were made in his addresses to the Italian Catholic Union of Midwives, October 29, 1951, and to the National Congress of the Family Front and the Association of Large Families, November 26, 1951. In these two addresses he explains the laws governing the use of the sterile period in woman; he treats about the morality of direct and indirect abortions; he states that upon married couples who perform the act peculiar to their state, nature and the Creator impose the function of helping the conservation of the human race; he points out the primary purpose of marriage; the blessings of parenthood; the possibility of, and in some cases the necessity of, complete sexual abstinence in marriage; the immorality of sterilization, modern hedonism, artificial insemination; and he touches briefly upon the education of children, sex instruction, and virginity.

In his speech on "Woman's Duties in Social and Political Life," Pius XII turns the spotlight on many facets of the feminine problem. He explains woman's dignity in the light of modern conditions; he treats about woman's place in the home, motherhood, and about the harmful consequences of woman's absence from the home; and he points out woman's obligation to participate in public life.

Pius XI indicated that there are many single women in the world, but Pius XII was the first pope who discussed the status of the bachelor girl, and he emphasized the need of special training for young girls.

CHRONOLOGICAL LIST OF PAPAL DOCUMENTS QUOTED; REFERENCES FOR ORIGINAL AND ENGLISH TEXTS

LEO XIII

1878, April 21: *Inscrutabili Dei,* an Encyclical Letter on the evils of society, given at St. Peter's, Rome, Easter Sunday, during the first year of Pope Leo XIII's Pontificate.
Original text in Latin: *Acta Sanctae Sedis,* 10:585–592.
English texts: *Ave Maria,* XIV (May 25, 1878), 327–331; *Dublin Review,* LXXXIII (July, 1878), 220–227; *Social Wellsprings,* Rev. Joseph Husslein, S.J. (Milwaukee: The Bruce Publishing Co., 1949), I, 2–11; *Tablet,* LI (May 4, 1878), 553–554; *The Great Encyclical Letters of Pope Leo XIII,* Rev. J. J. Wynne, S.J. (New York: Benziger Brothers, 1903), pp. 9–21; *The Pope and the People* (London: Catholic Truth Society, 28–40 Eccleston Square, 1932), pp. 1–11.

1878, December 28: *Quod Apostolici Muneris,* an Encyclical Letter on socialism, communism, and nihilism, given at St. Peter's, Rome, in the first year of Pope Leo XIII's Pontificate.
Original text in Latin: *Acta Sanctae Sedis,* 11:372–379.
English texts: *Ave Maria,* XV (February 15, 1879), 125–129; *Social Wellsprings,* Rev. Joseph Husslein, S.J. (Milwaukee: The Bruce Publishing Co., 1949), I, 14–23; *Tablet,* LIII (January 18, 1879), 71–74; *The Great Encyclical Letters of Pope Leo XIII,* Rev. J. J. Wynne, S.J. (New York: Benziger Brothers, 1903), pp. 22–33.

1880, February 10: *Arcanum,* an Encyclical Letter on Christian marriage, given at St. Peter's, Rome, in the second year of Pope Leo XIII's Pontificate.
Original text in Latin: *Acta Sancta Sedis,* 12:385–402.
English texts: *American Catholic Quarterly Review,* V (April, 1880), 332–345; *Social Wellsprings,* Rev. Joseph Husslein, S.J. (Milwaukee: The Bruce Publishing Co., 1949), I, 25–46; *The Great Encyclical Letters of Pope Leo XIII,* Rev. J. J. Wynne, S.J. (New York: Benziger Brothers, 1903), pp. 58–82; *The Pope and the People* (London: Catholic Truth Society, 28–40 Eccleston Square, 1932), pp. 23–44.

1884, February 8: *Nobilissima Gallorum Gens,* an Encyclical on the religious question in France, addressed to the Archbishops and Bishops of France, given in the sixth year of Pope Leo XIII's Pontificate.
Original text in Latin: *Acta Sanctae Sedis,* 16:241–248.
English text: *Tablet,* LXIII (February 6, 1884), 241–242.

1890, January 10: *Sapientiae Christianae,* an Encyclical Letter on the chief duties of Christian citizens, given at St. Peter's, Rome, in the twelfth year of Pope Leo XIII's Pontificate.

Original text in Latin: *Acta Sanctae Sedis*, 22:385–404.

English texts: *Social Wellsprings*, Rev. Joseph Husslein, S.J. (Milwaukee: The Bruce Publishing Co., 1949), I, 143–163; *Tablet*, LXXV (January 25, 1890), 121–126; *The Great Encyclical Letters of Pope Leo XIII*, Rev. J. J. Wynne, S.J. (New York: Benziger Brothers, 1903), pp. 180–207.

1891, May 15: *Rerum Novarum*, an Encyclical Letter on the condition of the workingman, given at St. Peter's, Rome, in the fourteenth year of Pope Leo XIII's Pontificate.

Original text in Latin: *Acta Sanctae Sedis*, 23:641–670.

English texts: *American Catholic Quarterly Review*, XVI (July, 1891), 529–557; *Catholic Mind*, XXIX (April 8, 1931), 145–180; *Five Great Encyclicals*, Rev. Gerald C. Treacy, S.J. (New York: The Paulist Press, 1941), pp. 1–30; *Social Wellsprings*, Rev. Joseph Husslein, S.J. (Milwaukee: The Bruce Publishing Co., 1949), I, 167–204; *The Condition of Labor* (Washington, D. C.: N.C.W.C., n.d.); *The Great Encyclical Letters of Pope Leo XIII*, Rev. J. J. Wynne, S.J. (New York: Benziger Brothers, 1903), pp. 208–248; *The Pope and the People* (London: Catholic Truth Society, 28–40 Eccleston Square, 1932), pp. 133–168.

PIUS X

1905, June 11: *Il Fermo Proposito*, an Encyclical on Christian social action, given to the Bishops of Italy, on the feast of Pentecost, the second year of Pope Pius X's Pontificate.

Original text in Italian: *Acta Sanctae Sedis*, 37:741–767.

English texts: *All Things in Christ*, Pius X, Rev. Vincent A. Yzermans (Minn.: Diocese of St. Cloud, 1952), pp. 44–53; *Tablet* CVI (July 8, 1905), 66–67 (extract); *The Pope and the People* (London: Catholic Truth Society, 28–40 Eccleston Square, 1932), pp. 189–201.

BENEDICT XV

1914, November 1: *Ad Beatissimi*, an Encyclical Letter in which the Pope appeals for peace, given at the outbreak of World War I, during the first year of Pope Benedict XV's Pontificate.

Original text in Latin: *Acta Apostolicae Sedis*, VI (November, 1914), 565–581.

English texts: *Acta Apostolicae Sedis*, VI (November 25, 1914), 647–660; *American Catholic Quarterly Review*, XXXIX (October, 1914), 656–668; *Catholic Mind*, XII (December 22, 1914), 731–752; *Catholic World*, C (January, 1915), 565–575; *Tablet*, CXXIV (December 12, 1914), 787–790; *The Pope and the People* (London: Catholic Truth Society, 28–40 Eccleston Square, 1932), pp. 202–217; *The Pope Speaks* (New York: Harcourt, Brace and Co., 1940), pp. 265–284.

1919, October 22: *Woman's Mission in Modern Society,* a discourse given by His Holiness in reply to the address presented by the Italian Catholic Women's Unit, given during the fifth year of Pope Benedict XV's Pontificate. Original text not located.

English texts: *Catholic Mind,* XVII (December 22, 1919), 453–457; *Tablet,* CXXXIV (November 1, 1919), 559–560.

1920, December 1: *Annus Iam Plenus,* an Encyclical Letter on the aid of child war victims, on the necessity of rendering further assistance to those children who owing to the war are in a state of urgent need, given at St. Peter's, Rome, during the seventh year of Pope Benedict XV's Pontificate.

Original text in Latin: *Acta Apostolicae Sedis,* XII (December 1, 1920), 553–556.

English texts: *Catholic Mind,* XIX (February 8, 1921), pp. 55–59; *Tablet,* CXXXVII (December 25, 1920), 872.

1921, January 6: *Sacra Propediem,* an Encyclical Letter on the seventh centenary of the Third Order of St. Francis, given near St. Peter's, Rome, on the feast of the Epiphany, in the seventh year of Pope Benedict XV's Pontificate.

Original text in Latin: *Acta Apostolicae Sedis,* XIII (January 24, 1921), 33–41.

English text: *Catholic Mind,* XIX (March 22, 1921), 101–109.

PIUS XI

1922, December 23: *Ubi Arcano,* an Encyclical Letter on the peace of Christ in the reign of Christ, given at St. Peter's, Rome, during the first year of Pope Pius XI's Pontificate.

Original text in Latin: *Acta Apostolicae Sedis,* XIV (December, 1922), 673–700.

English texts: *Papal Encyclicals and Letters of Pius XI* (London: Catholic Truth Society, 1932), pp. 2–46; *Social Wellsprings,* Rev. Joseph Husslein, S.J. (Milwaukee: The Bruce Publishing Company, 1949), II, 5–26; *Tablet,* CXLI (January 13, 1923), 36–42; *The Pope and the People* (London: Catholic Truth Society, 28–40 Eccleston Square, 1932), pp. 231–253; *The Pope Speaks* (New York: Harcourt, Brace and Co., 1940), pp. 296–311; *Ubi Arcano Dei* (Washington, D. C.: N.C.W.C., n.d.).

1929, December 31: *Rappresentanti in Terra, Divini Illius Magistri,* an Encyclical Letter on the Christian education of youth, given at St. Peter's, Rome, during the eighth year of Pope Pius XI's Pontificate.

Original text in Italian: *Acta Apostolicae Sedis,* XXI (December, 1929), 723–762.

English texts: *Catholic Educational Review,* XXVIII (March, 1930), 129–164; *Catholic Mind,* XXVIII (February 22, 1930), 61–91; *Catholic School Journal,* XXX (February, 1930), Suppl. 1–8; *Divini Illius Magistri* (Washington, D. C.: N.C.W.C., 1930); *Social Wellsprings,* Rev. Joseph Husslein, S.J. (Milwaukee: The Bruce Publishing Company, 1949), II, 89–121;

Ecclesiastical Review, LXXXII (April, 1930), 337–372; *Five Great Encyclicals,* Rev. Gerald C. Treacy, S.J. (New York: The Paulist Press, 1941), pp. 37–68; *Papal Encyclicals and Letters of Pius XI* (London: Catholic Truth Society, 1932), pp. 1–50.

1930, December 31: *Casti Connubii,* an Encyclical Letter on Christian marriage in our day, in view of the present conditions, needs, errors and vices that affect the family and society, given at St. Peter's, Rome, during the ninth year of Pope Pius XI's Pontificate.

Original text in Latin: *Acta Apostolicae Sedis,* XXII (December 31, 1930), 539–592.

English texts: *Casti Connubii* (Washington, D. C.: N.C.W.C., 1931); *Catholic Mind,* XXIX (January 22, 1931), 21–64; *Ecclesiastical Review,* LXXXIV (March, 1931), 225–264; *Five Great Encyclicals,* Rev. Gerald C. Treacy, S.J. (New York: The Paulist Press, 1941), pp. 77–117; *Social Wellsprings,* Rev. Joseph Husslein, S.J. (Milwaukee: The Bruce Publishing Company, 1949), II, 125–173; *Tablet,* CLVII (January 24, 1931), 125–136; *Papal Encyclicals and Letters of Pius XI* (Catholic Truth Society, 1932), pp. 1–67.

1931, May 15: *Quadragesimo Anno,* an Encyclical Letter on reconstructing the social order, in commemoration of the fortieth anniversary of the Encyclical *Rerum Novarum,* given at St. Peter's, Rome, during the tenth year of Pope Pius XI's Pontificate.

Original text in Latin: *Acta Apostolicae Sedis,* XXIII (June 1, 1931), 177–228.

English texts: *Catholic Mind,* XXIX (June 8, 1931), 257–306; *Ecclesiastical Review,* LXXXV (August, 1931), 113–158; *Five Great Encyclicals,* Rev. Gerald C. Treacy, S.J. (New York: The Paulist Press, 1941), pp. 125–168; *Papal Encyclicals and Letters of Pius XI* (London: Catholic Truth Society, 1932), pp. 1–70; *Quadragesimo Anno* (Washington, D. C.: N.C.W.C., 1931); *Reconstructing the Social Order* (New York: The American Press, n.d.); *Social Wellsprings,* Rev. Joseph Husslein, S.J. (Milwaukee: The Bruce Publishing Company, 1949), II, 178–234; *Tablet,* CLVII (June 6–20, 1931), 741–744, 790–794, 814–820.

1935, December 20: *Ad Catholici Sacerdotii,* an Encyclical Letter on the Catholic priesthood. The publication of this Encyclical coincided with the commemoration, in 1935, of the Jubilee of the Redemption, and the nineteenth centenary of the institution of the priesthood, given at St. Peter's, Rome, during the fourteenth year of Pope Pius XI's Pontificate.

Original text in Latin: *Acta Apostolicae Sedis,* XXVIII (January 2, 1936), 5–53.

English texts: *Catholic Mind,* XXXIV (February 8, 1936), 41–79; *Ecclesiastical Review,* XCIV (March, 1936), 262–295; *Social Wellsprings,* Rev. Joseph Husslein, S.J. (Milwaukee: The Bruce Publishing Company, 1949), II, 400–432; *The Catholic Priesthood* (Washington, D. C.: N.C.W.C., 1936).

1936, June 29: *Vigilanti Cura,* an Encyclical Letter on motion pictures, to the Archbishops and Bishops of the United States of America, and to other

Ordinaries, given at St. Peter's, Rome, on the feast of Saints Peter and Paul, in the fifteenth year of Pope Pius XI's Pontificate.
Original text in Latin: *Acta Apostolicae Sedis,* XXVIII (July 15, 1936), 249–263.
English texts: *Catholic Mind,* XXXIV (August 8, 1936), 305–317; *Ecclesiastical Review,* XCV (August, 1936), 113–125; *Motion Pictures* (Washington, D. C.: N.C.W.C., n.d.); *Social Wellsprings,* Rev. Joseph Husslein, S.J. (Milwaukee: The Bruce Publishing Company, 1949), II, 304–315; *Tablet,* CLXVIII (July 11, 1936), 49–52.

1937, March 14: *Mit brennender Sorge,* an Encyclical on the conditions of the Church in Germany, given on Passion Sunday, at St. Peter's, Rome, during the sixteenth year of Pope Pius XI's Pontificate.
Original text in German; *Acta Apostolicae Sedis,* XXIX (April 10, 1937), 145–167.
English texts: *Catholic Mind,* XXXV (May 8, 1937), 185–204; *Social Wellsprings,* Rev. Joseph Husslein, S.J. (Milwaukee: The Bruce Publishing Company, 1949), II, 318–338; *Tablet,* CLXIX (April 3, 1937), i–iv; *The Pope Speaks* (New York: Harcourt, Brace and Co., 1940), pp. 312–337.

1937, March 19: *Divini Redemptoris,* an Encyclical Letter on atheistic communism, given on the feast of St. Joseph, St. Peter's, Rome, in the sixteenth year of Pope Pius XI's Pontificate.
Original text in Latin: *Acta Apostolicae Sedis,* XXIX (March 31, 1937), 65–106.
English texts: *Catholic Mind,* XXXV (April 22, 1937), 141–174; *Ecclesiastical Review,* XCVI (May, 1937), 485–512; *Divini Redemptoris* (Washington, D. C.: N.C.W.C., March 19, 1937); *On Atheistic Communism* (London: Catholic Truth Society, 1937), pp. 52 ff.; *Social Wellsprings,* Rev. Joseph Husslein, S.J. (Milwaukee: The Bruce Publishing Company, 1949), II, 341–374; *Tablet,* CLXIX (March 27, 1937), Suppl. No. 5055.

1937, March 28: *Firmissimam Constantiam,* an Encyclical Letter on the Catholic Action plan for Mexico, given during the sixteenth year of Pope Pius XI's Pontificate.
Original text in Latin: *Acta Apostolicae Sedis,* XXIX (April 10, 1937), 189–199.
English texts: *Catholic Mind,* XXXV (May 22, 1937), 213–226; *Social Wellsprings,* Rev. Joseph Husslein, S.J. (Milwaukee: The Bruce Publishing Company, 1949), II, 376–388.

1937, September 29: *Ingravescentibus Malis,* an Encyclical Letter on peace through the rosary, given during the sixteenth year of Pope Pius XI's Pontificate.
Original text in Latin: *Acta Apostolicae Sedis,* XXIX (October 7, 1937), 373–380.
English texts: *Catholic Mind,* XXXV (November 8, 1937), 433–440; *Ingravescentibus Malis* (Washington, D. C.: N.C.W.C., n.d.); *Social Wellsprings,* Rev. Joseph Husslein, S.J. (Milwaukee: The Bruce Publishing Company, 1949), II, 391–397; *Tablet,* CLXX (October 9, 1937), 478–479; *The Holy Rosary* (London: Catholic Truth Society, 1937), pp. 1–12.

PIUS XII

1939, April 16: *Message Broadcast to Spain,* a message delivered by radio to the Spanish people, given during the first year of Pope Pius XII's Pontificate.
Original text in Spanish: *Acta Apostolicae Sedis,* XXXI (April 24, 1939), 151–154.
English text: *The Pope Speaks,* Charles Rankin, Most Rev. Edwin B. O'Hara (New York: Harcourt, Brace and Company, 1940), pp. 134–136.

1939, October 20: *Summi Pontificatus,* an Encyclical Letter on the function of the state in the modern world, given at Castel Gandolfo, near Rome, during the first year of Pope Pius XII's Pontificate.
Original text in Latin: *Acta Apostolicae Sedis,* XXXI (October 28, 1939), 413–453.
English texts: *Catholic Mind,* XXXVII (November 8, 1939), 890–918; *Ecclesiastical Review,* CI (December, 1939), 513–539; *Summi Pontificatus* (Washington, D. C.: N.C.W.C., 1939), pp. 1–48; *Summi Pontificatus* (New York: The Paulist Press, n.d.), pp. 1–32; *Tablet,* CLXXIV (November 11, 1939), 552–560; *The Pope Speaks,* Charles Rankin, Most Rev. Edwin V. O'Hara (New York: Harcourt, Brace and Company, 1940), pp. 148–194.

1939, November 1: *Sertum Laetitiae,* an Encyclical Letter to the Archbishops and Bishops on the one hundred and fiftieth anniversary of the establishment of the Ecclesiastical Hierarchy in the United States, given on the feast of All Saints, during the first year of Pope Pius XII's Pontificate.
Original text in Latin: *Acta Apostolicae Sedis,* XXXI (November 25, 1939), 635–644.
English texts: *Catholic Mind,* XXXVII (November 22, 1939), 923–940; *Ecclesiastical Review,* CI (December, 1939), 540–550; *Irish Ecclesiastical Record,* LV (February, 1940), 201–210; *Sertum Laetitiae* (New York: The Paulist Press, n.d.), pp. 1–23; *The Pope Speaks,* Charles Rankin, Most Rev. Edwin V. O'Hara (New York: Harcourt, Brace and Company, 1940), pp. 198–215.

1940, January 3 to October 23: *The Holy Father Speaks to Newlyweds,* a series of talks to newly married couples received in audience by Pope Pius XII, during the second year of his Pontificate.
Original text in Italian: *Scritti e Discorsi,* S.S. Pio XII (1940), Vol. II.
English text: *Holy Father Speaks to Newlyweds,* trs., Rev. Bernard Souse, O.S.B., and Rev. David Kinish, O.S.B., ed., Rev. Edgar Schmiedler, O.S.B. (Washington, D. C.: N.C.W.C., August 1, 1943), pp 1–56.

1941, October 3: "Marriage Legislation," an allocution given to the members of the Sacred Tribunal of the Roman Rota, during the third year of Pope Pius XII's Pontificate.
Original text in Italian: *Acta Apostolicae Sedis,* XXXIII (October 25, 1941), 421–426.
English texts: *Clergy Review,* XXII (February, 1942), 84–88; *The Unwearied Advocate,* Vincent A. Yzermans (Minnesota: St. Cloud, 25 Eighth Avenue So., 1954), I, 100–103.

1941, October 26: "Allocution to a Concourse of Women of Catholic Action," given on feast of Christ the King, during the third year of Pope Pius XII's Pontificate.
Original text in Italian: *Acta Apostolicae Sedis,* XXXIII (November 21, 1941), 450–458.
English texts: *Clergy Review,* XXII (March, 1942), 132–139; *Guiding Christ's Little Ones* (Washington, D. C.: N.C.W.C., n.d.), pp. 1–15; *The Unwearied Advocate,* Vincent A. Yzermans (Minnesota: St. Cloud, 25 Eighth Avenue So., 1954), I, 103–110.

1942, December 24: *The Holy Season of Christmas and Sorrowing Humanity,* a Christmas message, to the world, by radio, on the fundamental principles concerning the internal order of states and people, given during the fourth year of Pope Pius XII's Pontificate.
Original text in Italian: *Acta Apostolicae Sedis,* XXXV (January 26, 1942), 9–24.
English texts: *Catholic Mind,* XLI (January, 1943), 45–60; *Tablet,* CLXXXI (January 2, 1943), 4–6; *The Unwearied Advocate,* Vincent A. Yzermans (Minnesota: St. Cloud, 25 Eighth Avenue So., 1954), I, 144–157.

1943, December 24: *Christmas Message,* a radio message to the world, stating that war destroys personal initiative and makes orderly family life very difficult, given during the fifth year of Pope Pius XII's Pontificate.
Original text in Italian: *Acta Apostolicae Sedis,* XXXVI (January 20, 1944), 5–11.
English texts: *Catholic Mind,* XLII (February, 1944), 65–76; *International Order* (Washington, D. C.: N.C.W.C., n.d.), pp. 12–24; *The Unwearied Advocate,* Vincent A. Yzermans (Minnesota: St. Cloud, 25 Eighth Avenue So., 1954), I, 172–182.

1945, February 17: "The Sacraments," an allocution given to the Pastors of the city of Rome and to the Preachers for the Sacred Time of Lent: on the Sacraments, during the seventh year of Pope Pius XII's Pontificate.
Original text in Italian: *Acta Apostolicae Sedis,* XXXVII (February 28, 1945), 33–43.
English texts: *American Ecclesiastical Review,* CXIII (December, 1945), 464–474; *The Unwearied Advocate,* Vincent A. Yzermans (Minnesota: St. Cloud, 25 Eighth Avenue So., 1954), II, 3–11.

1945, July 14: "Responsibility of The Motion Picture Industry," an address to the members of the Hollywood Motion Picture Executive Committee: responsibility of the motion picture industry, given during the seventh year of Pope Pius XII's Pontificate.
Original text in English: Discorsi e Radiomessagi, VII, pp. 119–122.
English texts: *Tablet,* CLXXXVI (July 21, 1945), 32; *The Unwearied Advocate,* Vincent A. Yzermans (Minnesota: St. Cloud, 25 Eighth Avenue So., 1954), II, 32–33.

1945, August 15: "To the Working Women of Italy"; an address given to the Congress of Italian Catholic Women Workers in Rome: women in industry, during the seventh year of Pope Pius XII's Pontificate.

Original text in Italian: *Acta Apostolicae Sedis*, XXXVII (August 25, 1945), 212–216.

English texts: *Catholic Action*, XXVII (September, 1945), 4–5 (extract); *Tablet* CLXXXVI (August 25, 1945), 91 (extract); *The Unwearied Advocate*, Vincent A. Yzermans (Minnesota: St. Cloud, 25 Eighth Avenue So., 1954), II, 35–38.

1945, October 21: *Woman's Duties in Social and Political Life*, an address given to the Catholic Women of Rome on the duties of woman in social and political life, during the seventh year of Pope Pius XII's Pontificate.
Original text in Italian: *Acta Apostolicae Sedis*, XXXVII (December 28, 1945), 284–295.
English texts: *Catholic Mind*, XLIII (December, 1945), 705–716; *The Unwearied Advocate*, Vincent A. Yzermans (Minnesota: St. Cloud, 25 Eighth Avenue So., 1954), II, 50–58; *Your Destiny Is At Stake* (Washington, D. C.: N.C.W.C., n.d.), pp. 3–12.

1946, January 6: *Aid to Youth in the World Crisis*, an Encyclical in which the Holy Father appeals for the care of the world's destitute children, given in the eighth year of Pope Pius XII's Pontificate.
Original text in Latin: *Acta Apostolicae Sedis*, XXXVIII (January 23, 1946), 5–10.
English texts: *Catholic Mind*, XLIV (March, 1946), 129–133; *Tablet*, CLXXXVII (January 12, 1946), 19–20.

1946, February 20: "The Church-Foundation of Society," an allocution of the Holy Father at the Imposition of Birettas on the Newly Created Cardinals, given in Vatican City, during the eighth year of Pope Pius XII's Pontificate.
Original text in Italian: *Acta Apostolicae Sedis*, XXXVIII (April 1, 1946), 141–151.
English texts: *Catholic Mind*, XLIV (April 1, 1946), 193–203; *The Function of the Church* (Washington, D. C.: N.C.W.C., n.d.), pp. 3–11; *The Unwearied Advocate*, Vincent A. Yzermans (Minnesota: St. Cloud, 25 Eighth Avenue So., 1954), II, 70–78.

1946, October 6: *On Faith and Marriage*, an address to the Sacred Roman Rota, Civil and Ecclesiastical, given during the eighth year of Pope Pius XII's Pontificate.
Original text in Italian: *Acta Apostolicae Sedis*, XXXVIII (November 23, 1946), 391–397.
English texts: *Catholic Mind*, XLV (March, 1947), 129–136; *The Unwearied Advocate*, Vincent A. Yzermans (Minnesota: St. Cloud, 25 Eighth Avenue So., 1954), II, 108–113.

1947, September 11: *Papal Directives for the Women of Today*, an allocution to the Congress of the International Union of Catholic Women's Leagues, given at Rome, Italy, during the ninth year of Pope Pius XII's Pontificate.
Original text in French: *Acta Apostolicae Sedis*, XXXIX (November 7, 1947), 480–488.
English texts: *Catholic Action*, XXX (January, 1948), 17–19; *Papal Directives for the Women of Today* (Washington, D. C.: N.C.W.C., n.d.), pp. 2–8.

1948, October 6: *Education and the Modern Environment,* a radio address to the Inter-American Congress on Catholic Education held at La Paz, Bolivia, given during the tenth year of Pope Pius XII's Pontificate.

Original text in Spanish: *Acta Apostolicae Sedis,* XL (October 26, 1948), 465–468.

English text: *Catholic Mind,* XLVII (February, 1949), 118–121.

1949, January 31: "To the Eucharistic Congress at Cali in Colombia," a radio address to the Eucharistic Congress at Cali in Colombia, given during the eleventh year of Pope Pius XII's Pontificate.

Original text in Spanish: *Acta Apostolicae Sedis,* XLI (February 25, 1949), 76–79.

English texts: *Catholic Documents* (London: Salesian Press, Lurrey Lane, Battersea, S.W., 11, 1949), No. 2, pp. 1–3; *The Unwearied Advocate,* Vincent A. Yzermans (Minnesota: St. Cloud, 25 Eighth Avenue So., 1954), II, pp. 255–257.

1949, July 24: "Woman's Apostolate," an allocution to women of Italian Catholic Action: woman's apostolate, family and the formation of youth, given during the eleventh year of Pope Pius XII's Pontificate.

Original text in Italian: *Acta Apostolicae Sedis,* XLI (September 6, 1949), 415–421.

English texts: *Catholic Action,* XXXI (October, 1949), 18–20; *Catholic Mind,* XLVII (November, 1949), 685–690; *The Unwearied Advocate,* Vincent A. Yzermans (Minnesota: St. Cloud, 25 Eighth Avenue So., 1954), I, 19–24.

1949, September 4: *The Social Problem,* a radio address to the German Catholic Congress, Bochum, stating a five-point program for the reconstruction of the social order, given during the eleventh year of Pope Pius XII's Pontificate.

Original text in German: *Acta Apostolicae Sedis,* XLI (September 29, 1949), 458–462.

English texts: *Catholic Mind,* XLVII (November, 1949), 701–704; *Tablet,* CXCIV (September 10, 1949), 173–174; *The Unwearied Advocate,* Vincent A. Yzermans (Minnesota: St. Cloud, 25 Eighth Avenue So., 1954), III, 27–30.

1949, September 30: *To Catholic Doctors,* an address to the Fourth International Convention of Catholic Doctors, given at Castel Gandolfo, during the eleventh year of Pope Pius XII's Pontificate.

Original text in French: *L'Osservatore Romano,* LXXXIX (October 1, 1949), 1.

English texts: *Catholic Action,* XXXI (November, 1949), 19 (extract); *Catholic Mind,* XLVIII (April, 1950), 250–253; *Tablet,* CXCIV (October 8, 1949), 232 (extract); *The Unwearied Advocate,* Vincent A. Yzermans (Minnesota: St. Cloud, 25 Eighth Avenue So., 1954), III, 40–44.

1949, December 23: *Christmas Message,* in which the Holy Father reminds parents not to forget their spiritual duties in their efforts to support their family, given during the eleventh year of Pope Pius XII's Pontificate.

Original text in Italian: *L'Osservatore Romano,* LXXXIX (December 24, 1949), 1.

English texts: *Catholic Mind,* XLVIII (March, 1950), 180–188; *1949 Christmas Message* (Washington, D. C.: N.C.W.C., n.d.), pp. 3–11; *The Unwearied Advocate,* Vincent A. Yzermans (Minnesota: St. Cloud, 25 Eighth Avenue So., 1954), III, 58–67; *Vital Speeches,* XVI (January 1, 1950), 163–166.

1950, May 15: *Duty of Educators,* a brief proclaiming St. John de la Salle the Patron Saint of all teachers and student teachers, given during the twelfth year of Pope Pius XII's Pontificate.
Original text in Latin: *Acta Apostolicae Sedis,* XLII (July 22, 1950), 465.
English text: *Catholic Mind,* XLVIII (August, 1950), 511–512.

1950, June 3: *Production of Human Needs,* an address to the delegates of the Catholic International Congresses for Social Study (Fribourg Union) and Social Action (Saint Gall Union) held at Rome, given during the twelfth year of Pope Pius XII's Pontificate.
Original text in Italian: *Acta Apostolicae Sedis,* XLII (July 22, 1950), 485–488.
English texts: *Catholic Mind,* XLVIII (August, 1950), 507–510; *The Unwearied Advocate,* Vincent A. Yzermans (Minnesota: St. Cloud, 25 Eighth Avenue So., 1954), III, 85–88.

1950, August 5: *The Modern State,* an address given before the Eighth International Congress of Administrational Sciences, during the twelfth year of Pope Pius XII's Pontificate.
Original text in French: *L'Osservatore Romano,* XC (August 6, 1950), 1.
English texts: *Catholic Mind,* XLIX (July, 1951), 460–462; *Tablet,* CXCVI (August 26, 1950), 177; *The Unwearied Advocate,* Vincent A. Yzermans (Minnesota: St. Cloud, 25 Eighth Avenue So., 1954), III, 92–94.

1950, August 12: *Humani Generis,* an Encyclical Letter concerning the false opinions about Catholic doctrine, given at St. Peter's, Rome, during the twelfth year of Pope Pius XII's Pontificate.
Original text in Latin: *Acta Apostolicae Sedis,* XLII (September 2, 1950), 561–578.
English texts: *Catholic Action,* XXXII (October, 1950), 3 ff.; *Catholic Documents* (London: Salesian Press, Lurrey Lane, Battersea, S.W., 11, Epiphany, 1951), No. 3, pp. 28–39; *Catholic Mind,* XLVIII (November, 1950), 688–700; *Humani Generis* (New York: The Paulist Press, n.d.); *Humani Generis* (Washington, D. C.: N.C.W.C., n.d.), pp. 3–10; *Tablet,* CXCVI (September 2, 1950), 187–190.

1950, December 3: *The Role of Family Saving,* an allocution delivered to employers of the Savings Bank of Rome and a mixed group of workers and employers, given during the twelfth year of Pope Pius XII's Pontificate.
Original text not located.
English texts: *Catholic Mind,* XLIX (May, 1951), 330–331; *The Unwearied Advocate,* Vincent A. Yzermans (Minnesota: St. Cloud, 25 Eighth Avenue So., 1954), III, 108–109.

1951, July 2: *Problems of Rural Life,* an address to members of the International Catholic Congress on Rural Problems, given during the thirteenth year of

Pope Pius XII's Pontificate.

Original text in Italian: *Acta Apostolicae Sedis,* XLIII (August 11, 1951), 554–557.

English texts: *Catholic Mind,* XLIX (October, 1951), 708–711; *The Unwearied Advocate,* Vincent A. Yzermans (Minnesota: St. Cloud, 25 Eighth Avenue So., 1954), III, 140–143.

1951, September 15: *Ingruentium Malorum,* an Encyclical on the recitation of the Marian Rosary, given at St. Peter's, Rome, during the thirteenth year of Pope Pius XII's Pontificate.

Original text in Latin: *Acta Apostolicae Sedis,* XLIII (September 18, 1951), 577–582.

English texts: *Catholic Mind,* XLIX (December, 1951), 826–829; *Irish Ecclesiastical Record,* LXXVII (May, 1952, ser. 5), 387–390; *On Reciting the Rosary* (Washington, D. C.: N.C.W.C., n.d.), pp. 2–8.

1951, September 15: *On Educating Youth,* an address to the First International Congress of Teaching Sisters, given during the thirteenth year of Pope Pius XII's Pontificate.

Original text in Italian: *Acta Apostolicae Sedis,* XLIII (October 20, 1951), 738–744.

English texts: *Catholic Mind,* L (June, 1952), 376–380; *Counsel to Teaching Sisters* (Washington, D. C.: N.C.W.C., 1951), pp. 3–9; *The Unwearied Advocate,* Vincent A. Yzermans (Minnesota: St. Cloud, 25 Eighth Avenue So., 1954), III, 143–148.

1951, October 29: *Apostolate of the Midwife,* an address given to the Italian Catholic Union of Midwives on moral questions affecting married life, given during the thirteenth year of Pope Pius XII's Pontificate.

Original text in Italian: *Acta Apostolicae Sedis,* XLIII (December 20, 1951), 835–854.

English texts: *Catholic Documents* (London: Salesian Press, Lurrey Lane, Battersea, February, 1952), No. VI, pp. 1–16; *Catholic Mind,* L (January, 1952), 51–61; *Moral Questions Affecting Married Life* (Washington, D. C.: N.C.W.C., 1951), pp. 3–23; *The Unwearied Advocate,* Vincent A. Yzermans (Minnesota: St. Cloud, 25 Eighth Avenue So., 1954), III, 154–169.

1951, November 26: *Morality in Marriage,* an address on morality in marriage, given during the thirteenth year of Pope Pius XII's Pontificate.

Original text in Italian: *Acta Apostolicae Sedis,* XLIII (December 20, 1951), 855–860.

English texts: *Catholic Mind,* L (May, 1952), 307–311; *Irish Ecclesiastical Record,* LXXVII (January, 1952), 56–60; *Moral Questions Affecting Married Life* (Washington, D. C.: N.C.W.C., 1951), pp. 24–29; *The Unwearied Advocate,* Vincent A. Yzermans (Minnesota: St. Cloud, 25 Eighth Avenue So., 1954), III, 185–190.

1952, May 4: *The Blessed Virgin Mary,* a radio address to the First Marian Congress of South Africa, Durban, given during the fourteenth year of Pope Pius XII's Pontificate.

Original text in English: *Acta Apostolicae Sedis,* XLIV (January 3, 1952), 429–431.

English text: *Catholic Mind,* LI (February, 1953), 127–128.

1952, September 14: *To Austrian Catholics,* a radio address by the Holy Father to a national convention of Austrian Catholics in Vienna, given during the fourteenth year of Pope Pius XII's Pontificate.

Original text in German: *Acta Apostolicae Sedis,* XLIV (October 16, 1952), 789–793.

English texts: *Catholic Documents* (London: Salesian Press, Lurrey Lane, Battersea, 1953), No. 10, pp. 21–24; *Catholic Mind,* LI (January, 1953), 48–51.

1952, December 24: *1952 Christmas Message,* an address by the Holy Father on the evil consequences of the present social and economic conditions on society, given during the fourteenth year of Pope Pius XII's Pontificate.

Original text in Italian: *Acta Apostolicae Sedis,* XLV (January 16, 1953), 33–46.

English text: *Catholic Mind,* LI (February 22, 1953), 111–122.

1953, March 19: *Adult Education,* a discourse to the pupils and teachers for adult education, given during the fifteenth year of Pope Pius XII's Pontificate.

Original text in Italian: *Acta Apostolicae Sedis,* XLV (April 27, 1953), 230–238.

English text: *Catholic Documents* (London: Salesian Press, Lurrey Lane, Battersea), No. 11, pp. 24–30.

1953, April 13: *Psychotherapy and Religion,* an address to the Fifth International Congress of Psychotherapy and Clinical Psychology, given during the fifteenth year of Pope Pius XII's Pontificate.

Original text in French: *Acta Apostolicae Sedis,* XLV (May 30, 1953), 278–286.

English texts: *Catholic Mind,* LI (July, 1953), 428–435; *On Psychotherapy and Religion* (Washington, D. C.: N.C.W.C., 1953), pp. 3–12.

1953, April 19: *Allocution to the Pupils of the Don Bosco School,* an address given on Good Shepherd Sunday, during the fifteenth year of Pope Pius XII's Pontificate.

Original text in Italian: *Acta Apostolicae Sedis,* XLV (May 25, 1953), 296–298.

English text: *Catholic Documents* (London: Salesian Press, Lurrey Lane, Battersea, November, 1953), No. 13, pp. 4–6.

1953, December 24: *1953 Christmas Message,* a radio address on modern technology and peace, given during the fifteenth year of Pope Pius XII's Pontificate.

Original text in Italian: *Acta Apostolicae Sedis,* XLVI (January 16, 1954), 33–36.

English texts: *Catholic Mind,* LII (March, 1954), 174–183; *On Modern Technology and Peace* (Washington, D. C.: N.C.W.C., December 24, 1953), pp. 1–13.

Bibliography

BOOKS

Carlen, Sister M. Claudia, I.H.M., *A Guide to the Encyclicals of the Roman Pontiffs from Leo XIII to the Present, 1878–1937* (New York: The H. W. Wilson Company, 1939), p. 247.

────── *Guide to the Documents of Pius XII, 1939–1949* (Westminster, Md.: The Newman Press, 1951), p. 229.

Catholic Dictionary (New York: Catholic Encyclopedia, 1929), p. 29.

Cicognani, A. G., *Canon Law,* 2nd rev. ed. Authorized English version (Philadelphia: Dolphin Press, 1934), p. 84.

Cronin, John F., S.S., *Catholic Social Principles* (Milwaukee: The Bruce Publishing Company, 1950), pp. 56–59.

Faherty, William B., S.J., *The Destiny of Modern Woman* (Westminster, Md.: The Newman Press, 1950), pp. 36, 38, 47, 57–58, 62–63, 182–185.

Husslein, Joseph, S.J., *Social Wellsprings* (Milwaukee: The Bruce Publishing Co., 1949), Vol. I, pp. 1–46, 162–163, 173–175, 192. Vol. II, pp. 8–10, 92–118, 126–172, 203, 310, 332–334, 345, 352, 382–384, 427–429.

Koenig, Harry C., *Principles of Peace* (Washington: N.C.W.C., 1943), pp. 243–244.

Papal Encyclicals and Letters of Pius XI (London: Catholic Truth Society, 1932), pp. 1–50, 1–67, 1–70.

Pius XII, *Scritti e Discorsi* (Rome: Vaticana, 1940), Vol. II.

Rankin, Charles, and O'Hara, E. V., *The Pope Speaks* (New York: Harcourt, Brace and Co., 1940), pp. 134–136, 148–194, 198–215, 265–284, 296–311, 312–337.

The National Catholic Almanac for 1953 (Patterson, N. J.: St. Anthony's Guild, 1953), p. 46.

The Pope and the People (London: Catholic Truth Society, 1932), pp. 1–11, 23–44, 133–168, 189–201, 202–217, 231–253.

Treacy, Gerald, S.J., *Five Great Encyclicals* (New York: The Paulist Press, 1941), pp. 1–30, 37–67, 77–116, 125–168, 177–206.

Wynne, J. J., S.J., *The Great Encyclical Letters of Pope Leo XIII* (New York: Benziger Brothers, 1903), pp. 9–21, 22–23, 34–57, 58–82, 180–207, 208–248.

Yzermans, Vincent A., *All Things in Christ, Pius X* (Minnesota: Diocese of St. Cloud, 1952), pp. 44–53.

Yzermans, Vincent A., *The Unwearied Advocate* (Minnesota: St. Cloud, 25 Eighth Avenue So., 1954), II, pp. 9–10, 32–33, 35–37.

PERIODICALS

Benedict XV, "Ad Beatissimi," *Acta Apostolicae Sedis,* VI (November 25, 1914), 565–581, 647–660.

────── "Annus Iam Plenus," *Acta Apostolicae Sedis,* XII (December 1, 1920), 553–556.

—— "Sacra Propediem," *Acta Apostolicae Sedis,* XXIV (January 24, 1921), 33–41.

—— "Ad Beatissimi," *American Catholic Quarterly Review,* XXXIX (October, 1914), 656–668.

—— "Ad Beatissimi," *Catholic Mind,* XII (December 22, 1914), 731–752.

—— "Woman's Mission in Modern Society," *Catholic Mind,* XVII (December 22, 1919), 453–457.

—— "Annus Iam Plenus," *Catholic Mind,* XIX (February 8, 1921), 55–59.

—— "Sacra Propediem," *Catholic Mind,* XIX (March 22, 1921), 106–107.

—— "Ad Beatissimi," *Catholic World,* C (January, 1915), 565–575.

—— "Ad Beatissimi," *Tablet,* CXXIV (December 12, 1914), 787–790.

—— "Woman's Mission in Modern Society," *Tablet,* CXXXIV (November 1, 1919), 559–560.

—— "Annus Iam Plenus," *Tablet,* CXXXVII (December 25, 1920), 872.

Leo XIII, "Inscrutabili Dei," *Acta Sanctae Sedis,* X, 585–592.

—— "Quod Apostolici Muneris," *Acta Sanctae Sedis,* XI, 372–378.

—— "Arcanum," *Acta Sanctae Sedis,* XII, 385–402.

—— "Nobilissima Gallorum Gens," *Acta Sanctae Sedis,* XVI, 241–248.

—— "Sapientiae Christianae," *Acta Sanctae Sedis,* XXII, 385–404.

—— "Rerum Novarum," *Acta Sanctae Sedis,* XXIII, 641–670.

—— "Arcanum," *American Catholic Quarterly Review,* V (April, 1880), 346–361.

—— "Rerum Novarum," *American Catholic Quarterly Review,* XVI (July, 1891), 529–557.

—— "Inscrutabili Dei," *Ave Maria,* XIV (May 25, 1878), 327–331.

—— "Quod Apostolici Muneris," *Ave Maria,* XV (February 15, 1879), 125–129.

—— "Rerum Novarum," *Catholic Mind,* XXIX (April 8, 1931), 145–180.

—— "Inscrutabili Dei," *Dublin Review,* LXXXIII (July, 1878), 220–227.

—— "Inscrutabili Dei," *Tablet,* LI (May 4, 1878), 553–554.

—— "Quod Apostolici Muneris," *Tablet,* LIII (January 18, 1879), 71–74.

—— "Nobilissima Gallorum Gens," *Tablet,* LXIII (February 6, 1884), 241–242.

—— "Sapientiae Christianae," *Tablet,* LXXV (January 25, 1890), 121–126.

Pius X, "Il Fermo Proposito," *Acta Sanctae Sedis,* XXXVII, 741–767.

—— "Il Fermo Proposito," *Tablet,* CVI (July 8, 1905), 66–67.

Pius XI, "Ubi Arcano," *Acta Apostolicae Sedis,* XIV (December, 1922), 673–700.

—— "Rappresentanti in Terra," *Acta Apostolicae Sedis,* XXI (December, 1929), 723–762.

—— "Casti Connubii," *Acta Apostolicae Sedis,* XXII (December 31, 1930), 539–592.

—— "Quadragesimo Anno," *Acta Apostolicae Sedis,* XXIII (June 1, 1931), 177–228.

—— "Ad Catholici Sacerdotii," *Acta Apostolicae Sedis,* XXVIII (January 2, 1936), 5–53.

—— "Vigilanti Cura," *Acta Apostolicae Sedis,* XXVIII (July, 1936), 249–263.

174   BIBLIOGRAPHY

—— "Mit brennender Sorge," *Acta Apostolicae Sedis,* XXIX (April 10, 1937), 145–167.

—— "Divini Redemptoris," *Acta Apostolicae Sedis,* XXIX (March 31, 1937), 65–106.

—— "Firmissimam Constantiam," *Acta Apostolicae Sedis,* XXIX (April 10, 1937), 189–199.

—— "Ingravescentibus Malis," *Acta Apostolicae Sedis,* XXIX (October 7, 1937), 373–380.

—— "Rappresentanti in Terra," *Catholic Educational Review,* XXVIII (March, 1930), 129–164.

—— "Rappresentanti in Terra," *Catholic Mind,* XXVIII (February 22, 1930), 61–91.

—— "Casti Connubii," *Catholic Mind,* XXIX (January 22, 1931), 21–64.

—— "Quadragesimo Anno," *Catholic Mind,* XXIX (June 8, 1931), 257–306.

—— "Ad Catholici Sacerdotii," *Catholic Mind,* XXXIV (February 8, 1936), 41–79.

—— "Vigilanti Cura," *Catholic Mind,* XXXIV (August 8, 1936), 305–317.

—— "Mit brennender Sorge," *Catholic Mind,* XXXV (May 8, 1937), 185–204.

—— "Divini Redemptoris," *Catholic Mind,* XXXV (April 22, 1937), 141–174.

—— "Firmissimam Constantiam," *Catholic Mind,* XXXV (May 22, 1937), 213–226.

—— "Ingravescentibus Malis," *Catholic Mind,* XXXV (November 8, 1937), 373–380.

—— "Rappresentanti in Terra," *Catholic School Journal,* XXX (February, 1930), Suppl. 1–8.

—— "Rappresentanti in Terra," *Ecclesiastical Review,* LXXXII (April, 1930), 337–372.

—— "Casti Connubii," *Ecclesiastical Review,* LXXXIV (March, 1931), 225–264.

—— "Quadragesimo Anno," *Ecclesiastical Review,* LXXXV (August, 1931), 113–158.

—— "Ad Catholici Sacerdotii," *Ecclesiastical Review,* XCIV (March, 1936), 262–295.

—— "Vigilanti Cura," *Ecclesiastical Review,* XCV (August, 1936), 113–125.

—— "Divini Redemptoris," *Ecclesiastical Review,* XCVI (May, 1947), 485–512.

—— "Divini Redemptoris," *Irish Ecclesiastical Record,* XLIX (June, 1937), 643–663.

—— "Ubi Arcano," *Tablet,* CXLI (January 13, 1923), 36–42.

—— "Casti Connubii," *Tablet,* CLVII (January 24, 1931), 125–136.

—— "Quadragesimo Anno," *Tablet,* CLVII (June 6–20, 1931), 741, 744, 790–794, 814–820.

—— "Vigilanti Cura," *Tablet,* CLXVIII (July 11, 1936), 49–52.

—— "Mit brennender Sorge," *Tablet,* CLXVII (April 3, 1937), i–iv.

—— "Divini Redemptoris," *Tablet,* CLXIX (March 27, 1937), Suppl. No. 5055.

———— "Ingravescentibus Malis," *Tablet*, CLXX (October 9, 1937), 478–479.

Pius XII, "Message Broadcast to Spain," *Acta Apostolicae Sedis*, XXIV (April 24, 1939), 151–154.

———— "Summi Pontificatus," *Acta Apostolicae Sedis*, XXXI (October 28, 1939), 413–453.

———— "Sertum Laetitiae," *Acta Apostolicae Sedis*, XXXI (November 25, 1939), 635–644.

———— "Marriage Legislation," *Acta Apostolicae Sedis*, XXXIII (October 25, 1941), 421–426.

———— "Allocution to a Concourse of Women of Catholic Action," *Acta Apostolicae Sedis*, XXXIII (November 21, 1941), 450–458.

———— "1942 Christmas Message," *Acta Apostolicae Sedis*, XXXV (January 26, 1943), pp. 9–24.

———— "Christmas Message," *Acta Apostolicae Sedis*, XXXVI (January 20, 1944), 11–24.

———— "The Sacraments," *Acta Apostolicae Sedis*, XXXVII (February 28, 1945), 33–43.

———— "To the Working Women of Italy," *Acta Apostolicae Sedis*, XXXVII (August 25, 1945), 212–216.

———— "Woman's Duties in Social and Political Life," *Acta Apostolicae Sedis*, XXXVII (December 28, 1945), 284–295.

———— "Aid to Youth," *Acta Apostolicae Sedis*, XXXVIII (January 23, 1946), 5–10.

———— "The Church — Foundation of Society," *Acta Apostolicae Sedis*, XXXVIII (April 1, 1946), 141–151.

———— "On Faith and Marriage," *Acta Apostolicae Sedis*, XXXVIII (November 23, 1946), 391–397.

———— "Papal Directives for the Women of Today," *Acta Apostolicae Sedis*, XXXIX (November 7, 1947), 480–488.

———— "Education and the Modern Environment," *Acta Apostolicae Sedis*, XL (October 26, 1948), 465–468.

———— "To the Eucharistic Congress at Cali in Colombia," *Acta Apostolicae Sedis*, XLI (February 25, 1949), 76–79.

———— "Woman's Apostolate," *Acta Apostolicae Sedis*, XLI (September 6, 1949), 415–421.

———— "The Social Problem," *Acta Apostolicae Sedis*, XLI (September 29, 1949), 458–462.

———— "Duty of Educators," *Acta Apostolicae Sedis*, XLII (July 22, 1950), 465.

———— "Production of Human Needs," *Acta Apostolicae Sedis*, XLII (July 22, 1950), 485–488.

———— "Humani Generis," *Acta Apostolicae Sedis*, XLII (September 2, 1950), 561–578.

———— "Problems of Rural Life," *Acta Apostolicae Sedis*, XLIII (August 11, 1951), 554–557.

———— "On Reciting the Rosary," *Acta Apostolicae Sedis*, XLIII (September 18, 1951), 577–582.

―――― "Counsel to Teaching Sisters," *Acta Apostolicae Sedis*, XLIII (October 20, 1951), 738–744.

―――― "Apostolate of the Midwife," *Acta Apostolicae Sedis*, XLIII (December 20, 1951), 835–854.

―――― "Morality in Marriage," *Acta Apostolicae Sedis*, XLIII (December 20, 1951), 855–860.

―――― "The Blessed Virgin Mary," *Acta Apostolicae Sedis*, XLIV (January 3, 1952), 429–431.

―――― "To Austrian Catholics," *Acta Apostolicae Sedis*, XLIV (October 16, 1952), 789–793.

―――― "1952 Christmas Message," *Acta Apostolicae Sedis*, XLV (January 16, 1953), 33–46.

―――― "Adult Education," *Acta Apostolicae Sedis*, XLV (April 27, 1953), 230–238.

―――― "Allocution to the Pupils of the Don Bosco School," *Acta Apostolicae Sedis*, XLV (May 25, 1953), 296–298.

―――― "Psychotherapy and Religion," *Acta Apostolicae Sedis*, XLV (May 30, 1953), 278–286.

―――― "1953 Christmas Message," *Acta Apostolicae Sedis*, XLV (January 16, 1954), 33–36.

―――― "To the Working Women of Italy," *Catholic Action*, XXVII (September, 1945), 4–5 (extract).

―――― "Papal Directives for the Women of Today," *Catholic Action*, XXX (January, 1948), 17–19.

―――― "Woman's Apostolate," *Catholic Action*, XXXI (October, 1949), 18–20.

―――― "To Catholic Doctors," *Catholic Action*, XXXI (November, 1949), 19 (extract).

―――― "Humani Generis," *Catholic Action*, XXXII (October, 1950), p. 3 ff.

―――― "To the Eucharistic Congress at Cali in Colombia," *Catholic Documents*, No. 2 (January 31, 1949), 1–3.

―――― "Humani Generis," *Catholic Documents*, No. 3 (Epiphany, 1951), pp. 28–39.

―――― "Apostolate of the Midwife," *Catholic Documents*, No. 11 (February, 1952), pp. 1–16.

―――― "To Austrian Catholics," *Catholic Documents*, No. 10 (1952), pp. 21–24.

―――― "Adult Education," *Catholic Documents*, No. 11 (1953), pp. 24–30.

―――― "Allocution to the Pupils of the Don Bosco School," *Catholic Documents*, No. 13 (November, 1953), pp. 5–6.

―――― "Summi Pontificatus," *Catholic Mind*, XXXVII (October 22, 1939), 890–918.

―――― "Sertum Laetitiae," *Catholic Mind*, XXXVII (1939), 923–940.

―――― "1942 Christmas Message," *Catholic Mind*, XLI (January, 1943), pp. 45–60.

―――― "Christmas Message," *Catholic Mind*, XLII (February, 1944), 65–76.

―――― "Woman's Duties in Social and Political Life," *Catholic Mind*, XLIII (December, 1945), 705–716.

——— "Quemadmodum," *Catholic Mind*, XLIV (March, 1946), 129–133.

——— "The Church — Foundation of Society," *Catholic Mind*, XLIV (April, 1946), 193–203.

——— "On Faith and Marriage," *Catholic Mind*, XLV (March, 1947), 129–136.

——— "Education and the Modern Environment," *Catholic Mind*, XLVII (February, 1949), 118–121.

——— "Woman's Apostolate," *Catholic Mind*, XLVII (November, 1949), 685–690.

——— "The Social Problem," *Catholic Mind*, XLVII (November, 1949), 701–704.

——— "To Catholic Doctors," *Catholic Mind*, XLVIII (April, 1950), pp. 250–253.

——— "Christmas Message, 1949," *Catholic Mind*, XLVIII (March, 1950), 180–188.

——— "Duty of Educators," *Catholic Mind*, XLVIII (August, 1950), 511–512.

——— "Production of Human Needs," *Catholic Mind*, XLVIII (August, 1950), 507–510.

——— "Humani Generis," *Catholic Mind*, XLVIII (November, 1950), 688–700.

——— "The Role of Family Saving," *Catholic Mind*, XLIX (May, 1951), 330–331.

——— "The Modern State," *Catholic Mind*, XLIX (July, 1951), 460–462.

——— "Problems of Rural Life," *Catholic Mind*, XLIX (October, 1951), 708–711.

——— "On Reciting the Rosary," *Catholic Mind*, XLIX (December, 1951), 826–829.

——— "Apostolate of the Midwife," *Catholic Mind*, L (January, 1952), 51–61.

——— "Morality in Marriage," *Catholic Mind*, L (May, 1952), 307–311.

——— "Counsel to Teaching Sisters," *Catholic Mind*, L (June, 1952), 376–380.

——— "To Austrian Catholics," *Catholic Mind*, LI (January, 1953), 48–51.

——— "The Blessed Virgin Mary," *Catholic Mind*, LI (February, 1953), 127–128.

——— "Christmas Message, 1952," *Catholic Mind*, LI (February 22, 1953), 111–122.

——— "Psychotherapy and Religion," *Catholic Mind*, LI (July, 1953), 428–435.

——— "Christmas Message, 1953," *Catholic Mind*, LII (March, 1954), 174–183.

——— "Marriage Legislation," *Clergy Review*, XXII (February, 1942), 84–88.

——— "Allocution to a Concourse of Women of Catholic Action," *Clergy Review*, XXII (March, 1942), 132–138.

——— "Responsibility of The Motion Picture Industry," *Discorsi e Radiomessagi*, 1945, VII, 119–122.

——— "Summi Pontificatus," *Ecclesiastical Review*, CI (December, 1939), 513–539.

——— "Sertum Laetitiae," *Ecclesiastical Review*, CI (December, 1939), 540–550.

——— "The Sacraments," *Ecclesiastical Review*, CXIII (December, 1945), 464–474.

——— "Sertum Laetitiae," *Irish Ecclesiastical Record*, LV (February, 1940), 201–210.

—— "Morality in Marriage," *Irish Ecclesiastical Record*, LXXVII (January, 1952), 56–60.

—— "On Reciting the Rosary," *Irish Ecclesiastical Record*, LXXVII (May, 1952), ser. 5, 387–390.

—— "Summi Pontificatus," *Tablet*, CLXXIV (November 11, 1939), 552–560.

—— "1942 Christmas Message," *Tablet*, CLXXXI (January 2, 1943), pp. 4–6.

—— "Responsibility of The Motion Picture Industry," *Tablet*, CLXXXVI (July 21, 1945), 32.

—— "To the Working Women of Italy," *Tablet*, CLXXXVI (August 25, 1945), 91 (extract).

—— "Quemadmodum," *Tablet*, CLXXXVII (January 12, 1946), 19–20.

—— "The Social Problem," *Tablet*, CXCIV (September 10, 1949), 173–174.

—— "To Catholic Doctors," *Tablet*, CXCIV (October 8, 1949), 232 (extract).

—— "The Modern State," *Tablet*, CXCVI (August 26, 1950), 177.

—— "Humani Generis," *Tablet*, CXCVI (September 10, 1950), 187–190.

—— "1949 Christmas Message," *Vital Speeches*, XVI (January 1, 1950), pp. 163–166.

PAMPHLETS

Leo XIII, *Christian Marriage*, Rev. G. C. Treacy, S.J. (New York: The Paulist Press, 1942).

—— *The Condition of Labor* (Washington: N.C.W.C., n.d.).

Pius XI, *Atheistic Communism* (London: Catholic Truth Society, 1937).

—— *Divini Illius Magistri* (Washington: N.C.W.C., 1930).

—— *Divini Redemptoris* (Washington: N.C.W.C., March 19, 1937).

—— *Ingravescentibus Malis* (Washington: N.C.W.C., n.d.).

—— *Motion Pictures* (Washington: N.C.W.C., n.d.).

—— *Quadragesimo Anno* (Washington: N.C.W.C., 1931).

—— *Reconstructing the Social Order* (New York: The America Press, n.d.).

—— *The Catholic Priesthood* (Washington: N.C.W.C., 1936).

—— *The Holy Rosary* (London: Catholic Truth Society, 1937).

—— *Ubi Arcano Dei* (Washington: N.C.W.C., n.d.).

Pius XII, *Christmas Message, 1949* (Washington: N.C.W.C., n.d.).

—— *Counsel to Teaching Sisters* (Washington: N.C.W.C., 1951).

—— *Guiding Christ's Little Ones* (Washington: N.C.W.C., n.d.).

—— *Humani Generis* (New York: Paulist Press, n.d.).

—— *Humani Generis* (Washington: N.C.W.C., n.d.).

—— *Moral Questions Affecting Married Life* (Washington: N.C.W.C., 1951).

—— *On Modern Technology and Peace* (Washington: N.C.W.C., December 24, 1953).

—— *On Reciting the Rosary* (Washington: N.C.W.C., n.d.).

—— *Papal Directives for the Women of Today* (Washington: N.C.W.C., n.d.).

—— *Psychotherapy and Religion* (Washington: N.C.W.C., April 13, 1953).

—— *Sertum Laetitiae* (Washington: N.C.W.C., 1939).

———— *Summi Pontificatus* (New York: The Paulist Press, n.d.).

———— *The Function of the Church* (Washington: N.C.W.C., n.d.).

———— *The Holy Father Speaks to Newlyweds* (Washington: The Family Life Bureau, N.C.W.C., 1943).

———— *Your Destiny Is At Stake* (Washington: N.C.W.C., n.d.).

NEWSPAPERS

Pius XII, "To Catholic Doctors," *L'Osservatore Romano,* LXXXIX (October 1, 1949), 1.

———— "Christmas Message," *L'Osservatore Romano,* LXXXIX (December 24, 1949), 1.

———— "The Modern State," *L'Osservatore Romano,* XC (August 6, 1950), 1.

INDEX OF PAPAL DOCUMENTS
AS GIVEN IN THE CHRONOLOGICAL LIST

GENERAL INDEX

Abortion, immorality of, 77 ff
Abstinence, grave risk to motherhood and, 70 f; marriage and, 71 ff
Acta Leonis, ix
Ad Beatissimi, on contempt for authority, 124
Ad Catholici Sacerdotii, on ideal Christian home, 138 f; vocation to priesthood, 101 f
Adultery, 18 ff
Affection, mutual, 111 f
Aged, care of the, 139
Aid to Youth in the World Crisis, on delinquency, 110
Allocution to the Pupils of the Don Bosco School, on education of youth, 100
Annus Iam Plenus, on training in charity, 125
Apostolate of the Midwife, on abortion and unborn child, 79 f; abstinence and grave risk of motherhood, 70 f; on abstinence in marriage, 73 f; on artificial insemination, 85 f; on baptism, 110 f; on chastity, 103; on conjugal love, 113 f; on conjugal relations, 67 f; on end of marriage, 63; on euthanasia, 84; on immorality of sterilization, 77; on marriage as state of life, 63 f; on mutual affection, 111 f; on obligations to control passions, 67; on parenthood, 87 ff; on reasons for using sterile period, 69 f; on sex education, 108; on sexual act, 64 f; on sexual pleasure, 65; on use of sterile period, 68 f
Arcanum, on authority of Church over marriage, 23 ff; on benefits of marriage, 114 f; on care of children, 109; on Church and civil authority in marriage, 27 f; on civil marriage, 35; on condemnation of divorce, 47 f; on conjugal fidelity, 16; on corruption of marriage by Gentiles, 2 f; on corruption of marriage by Jews, 3 f; on

dangers of mixed marriage, 32 f; on dignity of marriage, 7; on divorce and secularization of marriage, 45 ff; on evils of unhallowed marriage, 116 f; on indissolubility of marriage, 12; on instruction in marriage, 57; on marriage of nonbaptized, 6; on marriage as a sacrament, 6 f; on mutual duties of husband and wife, 111; on mutual life of husband and wife, 20 f; on origins of marriage, 1 f; on procreation, 61; on religion and happiness in marriage, 112; on sacredness of marriage, 4; on secularization of marriage, 36 ff; on unity of marriage, 11
Artificial insemination, *see* Insemination
To Austrian Catholics, on civil marriage, 35; on education of youth, 100
Authority, contempt for, 124; paternal, 138

Baptism, duty of, 110 f
Benedict XV, on contempt for authority, 124; letter to Canon Nury, x; letter to Clara Douglas Sherman, x; letter to Mother Angela of Our Lady, x; on modesty, 127 f; on religious education of children, 90; summary of teachings on family and marriage, 156; on training in charity, 125; woman as man's co-worker, x; on woman's apostolate, 131 f
Birth control, artificial, 73 ff; evils of, 73 ff

Casti Connubii, on abortion, 80 f; on adultery, 18 ff; on benefits of stability of marriage, 15 f; on care of children, 109 f; on character training, 103 f; on children as blessing in marriage, 115; on choosing a partner in marriage, 60; on Church as guide, 31; on Church laws on mixed marriage, 33 f; on civil authority and Church in

183